AF515497

The Good Citizen

A parenting journey that transforms children into responsible citizens.

Dr Mohamed Nismy Rafiudeen, PhD

PUBLICATION DATA
Name: The Good Citizen (Novel)
ISBN:
First edition: September 2024
Written and published by Mohamed Nismy Rafiudeen
Cover design by Mus'ab Mohamed Nismy
Disclaimer: Copyright @2024 Mohamed Nismy Rafiudeen
All rights reserved. No part of this book may be reproduced or used in any manner without the prior written permission of the copyright owner, except for the use of brief quotations in a book review. To request permission, contact the publisher.

Table of Contents

FOREWORD

Welcome to a journey of growth, leadership, and wisdom! This book goes beyond simple storytelling—it offers valuable lessons in parenting, personal development, and community leadership, all inspired by the rich teachings of Islam.

At the heart of this book is a story that speaks directly to the minds and hearts of parents, youth, and community leaders. Readers will be entertained by the main character, Siddique's captivating journey and get insights to enhance their roles. The tale's hero, a child much like any other, navigates life's challenges with courage and faith, learning valuable lessons. Each chapter contains examples of good character and leadership, from showing kindness and respect to others to developing resilience in the face of difficulties.

Parents will find inspiration in how the child's guardians provide gentle guidance, balance discipline with love, foster independence, and nurture the child's spiritual and emotional growth. The parenting style modelled in this story offers valuable lessons for families striving to raise children with strong moral foundations and leadership qualities, all guided by the principles of Islam.

What makes this story truly unique is that it goes beyond the adventure. The way the child is parented in this story adds an extra layer of richness, making it a book for parents and a meaningful read for children. By following this character's journey, children will be inspired to develop their personalities, gain the confidence to stand up for what is right and lead others by example.

This book offers something for everyone. Parents will appreciate the deep lessons on parenting and values, children will be drawn in by the story's excitement and personal growth, and adults will have a role model in community work. The story touches on what it means to grow into a responsible, caring individual with a solid moral compass shaped by faith. In the end, the author provides self-assessment tools as a reflection of the story to help all the readers, including parents, youth, and community workers/leaders, assess their current status and determine the areas that need improvement.

As you read through these pages, whether a child or an adult, I hope you will find joy, inspiration, and a renewed sense of purpose in living by Islam's timeless values.

This is a story that not only entertains but enriches the hearts and minds of all who read it.

Dr Rayes Musthafa, MD

Consultant Paediatrician
Chairman Abrar Foundation

PREFACE

In the name of Allah, the Most Merciful, who has guided me to undertake this work, even though I had no prior experience in writing.

May Allah's eternal peace and blessings be upon the Messenger of Allah (SAW), who showed us the path to success in this life and the hereafter.

I am deeply thankful to Allah for the positive social changes we are witnessing today and the emergence of a socially conscious and cultured generation. This change results from various individuals and organisations' years of dedicated social work.

I respectfully remember those who worked tirelessly to make this possible.

Because of their sacrifices and efforts, we can now think about reforming our lives and the society around us. They set aside their personal lives to ensure a better future for us.

May Allah forgive any mistakes they made, knowingly or unknowingly, and may they be fully rewarded for their efforts on the Day of Judgment. Ameen.

Today, we see a growing awareness of Islam everywhere. Even more, non-Muslims are seeking to learn about Islam each day. Alhamdulillah!

This raises a critical question: What role should we play in this positive change?

Should we remain as spectators, or should we step up and take responsibility?

As Muslims who understand the purpose of this worldly life and the joys of the afterlife, we cannot simply stand by. We must consider our role and find ways to increase our contributions to society.

Dear parents, Allah's grace has blessed you with children. Have you ever considered how you can use this blessing to make a meaningful contribution to social progress?

Dear young brothers and sisters, you are in a unique phase of life filled with energy and potential. Have you ever considered how you can use this time to better society?

This book is a humble attempt to share my thoughts, efforts, and experiences in seeking answers to these questions.

When we think about community development, one of the main challenges we face is the lack of strong, principled leaders.

Even though many efforts are made to develop leadership skills at different levels, the results are often less effective than they could be.

It is often said that "a good family is a living university."

The family environment is a wonderful arrangement created by Allah. If parents are properly guided, they can raise great leaders for our society. This book attempts to bring this idea to life.

We also need to address the many youth who live without meaningful ambitions. Recognising their talents, guiding them, and encouraging them to become effective contributors, especially during their school and university years, is essential. This book aims to offer an inspiring model for such youth.

Additionally, many who are engaged in social work today tend to focus on short-term projects. Broader ideals must guide them; this book provides a role model.

I don't know what this write-up might be called in literary terms, but if you, the reader, can reflect on the points mentioned above, that is sufficient for me, Alhamdulillah.

The story in this book revolves around a personality named Siddique, who devoted his life to the revival of society. A foreigner who greatly admired him heard about his passing and rushed from abroad to attend his funeral. However, he arrived after the funeral had already taken place.

This foreigner had met Siddique once and had learned about the positive changes happening in the community. However, he did not know much about Siddique's life experiences, which deeply troubled him.

At the gravesite, he meets an elderly man deep in prayer, and they get to know each other. They have a long and meaningful conversation, during which they share many old memories—these memories from the content of this work.

The book consists of five chapters.

The journey of this book begins with *Chapter 1: SEED*, where the author encounters an old man, setting the stage for the story. Their brief exchange leads to the narration of the old man's story in the following three chapters.

Chapter 2: ROOT delves into the parenting experiences of Siddique's parents, offering valuable insights for parents who aspire to create a nurturing and productive environment for their children.

Chapter 3: SPROUT focuses on Siddique's youth, highlighting his teenage years, the discovery of his life mission, and his university experiences. This chapter emphasises the impact of strong parenting and the importance of preparation for future leadership roles, providing key takeaways for young readers.

Chapter 4: TREE showcases Siddique's contributions as a responsible citizen. It illustrates how he strategically turned challenges into opportunities, guiding his community towards a vision of a flourishing nation.

Finally, Chapter 5: LESSONS LEARNED includes self-assessment questions, allowing readers to reflect on the lessons from the previous chapters and apply them to their own lives.

May Allah reward all those who have contributed to the creation and publication of this work. May He grant us a permanent home in the beautiful paradise He has prepared for His servants. Ameen.

Dr Muhammad Nismy Rafiudeen, PhD
Human Resource Development Strategist

THE SEED

In the quiet courtyard of the mosque, people were gathered, talking anxiously. They told me that the funeral had already been taken to the cemetery.

My heart sank as I realised I had missed the funeral. I wanted to go near the burial place, but the crowd was so dense that it was almost impossible to move forward.

I pushed my way through the crowd, taking small, careful steps. It was like trying to wade through a thick sea of people.

After much effort and many apologies, I finally managed to get close to the grave. When I arrived, they were already sprinkling soil over it.

Around the grave, many people stood with worried faces.

Some were intensely focused on their prayers, their heads bowed and their hands raised.

Others had red, tear-streaked faces, showing how much they were hurting. They seemed lost in their thoughts, remembering the moments they had shared with the departed.

I, too, was deeply affected by the scene. I recalled the two days I had spent with that nobleman.

He shared many essential lessons with me, and those moments profoundly impacted my life.

As I stood there, I could feel my heart breaking. The thought of never seeing him again was almost too much to bear.

It was a very emotional and challenging time for me as I tried to come to terms with his loss.

The sadness in the air was almost palpable, and it seemed like the whole world had paused to mourn the passing of this remarkable person.

Only Allah and I could truly understand the deep anxiety that weighed on my heart.

I felt tears roll down my face as I stood by the grave, feeling utterly alone in my grief.

Soon, the crowd began to disperse, and people left quietly. Before long, only an old man and I remained beside the grave.

The elderly man looked to be around eighty years old. He was deeply engrossed in his prayers, his voice soft and filled with sorrow.

His grey beard was wet with tears, and he seemed to be pouring out his heart to Allah.

After a while, he tried to stand, but he struggled. His movements were slow and labored.

He looked at me with questioning eyes as if asking for help. Without hesitation,

I understood what he needed. I moved towards him, gently took his hands in mine, and helped him to his feet.

His gratitude was evident in his eyes as he looked at me with relief and appreciation.

In that quiet moment, we shared an unspoken connection, both bound by the grief of our loss.

The old man looked at me with gratitude, his eyes softening. He clasped my hands and said, "May Allah reward you with goodness." His voice was filled with sincerity.

"Brother!" he said with a curious tone, "You seem new to this town. Who are you?"

I introduced myself briefly, hoping to clarify my situation.

When I told him I had come straight from the airport hoping to attend the funeral prayer but had missed it, his expression changed to one of concern.

He asked with a heavy, compassionate voice, "You travelled such a long distance to be here! What was your relationship with him?"

I replied, "The changes happening in this town are truly remarkable. I wanted to see and learn from them. Two years ago, I had the opportunity to visit this town, and Allah blessed me with the chance to meet Brother Siddique and witness the incredible transformation he had brought about."

The old man listened intently, his eyes reflecting understanding and empathy.

"I had hoped to meet him again and hear about his life experiences, but I missed that chance. May Allah forgive me for my mistake."

Upon hearing this, the old man's face, filled with worry, suddenly brightened. He embraced me warmly, and I felt his tears of joy wet my shirt.

I asked him, "Uncle, what is your relationship with him? Do you know much about him?"

With a smile and nod, he replied while holding my hands, "The only regret I have is that he wasn't born as my son. But he is like my child—he is my sister's son. I watched him grow up and achieve great things in his life!"

The old man's eyes filled with tears as he continued, "Even his father didn't have the privilege I had."

"From his birth until now, I have witnessed all his actions and achievements, Alhamdulillah."

As I watched, I could see worry clouding the old man's face once more.

He quickly brushed away his tears and took a deep breath.

"Brother," he said softly, "knowing all his deeds brings me immense joy."

Hearing this, I felt relief and happiness wash over me. My desire to learn more about Brother Siddique's life seemed within reach.

The old man gently took my hands and suggested, "Let's go and sit under that big tree for some shade."

We walked slowly toward a tree, taking time and praising Allah with every step. Once we reached the shade, the old man settled gracefully on one of the tree's sprawling roots.

He raised his arms high, his voice filled with reverence as he prayed:

"Ya Allah! The crowd gathered here shows that Your servant Siddique devoted himself entirely to Your service. I witness this and pray that You, too, bear witness."

"Ya Allah! Include him among the righteous who lived and died for You."

"Please take care of his journey to the afterlife. Ameen."

His prayer, full of faith and devotion, resonated deeply with me. It felt like a fitting tribute to a life well-lived and a heartfelt plea for continued blessings.

THE ROOT

The mosque was bustling with activity as worshippers completed their prayers, their whispered supplications fading into a serene quiet.

Gradually, people began to leave, one by one, until the mosque was nearly empty.

Only Abdullah remained, deeply absorbed in his *sujud* (prostration). His forehead touched the cool ground, and he lingered there.

It was a moment of solitude, yet he was not alone; he was in a profound conversation with his Creator, seeking guidance and pouring out his soul.

I waited patiently for him. "Should I, who have waited so long, give up hope and walk away?" I pondered.

I was torn between the impulse to leave and the desire to stay, but something in me knew I needed to wait for him.

Finally, after what felt like an eternity, Abdullah gently rose from his position. His movements were slow and deliberate as if savouring the sacred moments of his prayer.

As he turned toward me, tears shimmered on his cheeks, a testament to the depth of his prayer.

His face bore a look of deep responsibility, as if he carried the world's weight on his shoulders, a reflection of someone who understood the gravity of his duties.

When I greeted him with "Assalamu Alaikum," his face softened, and a warm smile spread across his lips. He returned the greeting with genuine affection.

He eagerly reached for his mobile phone as if anticipating something important. He quickly checked a new message, and his face lit up joyfully within seconds.

His eyes sparkled as he looked at me, revealing that he had received good news from the doctor. A moment of relief and happiness seemed to fill the mosque with light.

Abdullah and I have been friends since childhood. From a very young age, he was drawn to faith and spirituality. People admired him for his gentle nature and exemplary character.

His knowledge of Islamic teachings, principles, and history was extensive, and he was always eager to learn more.

The Village Development Council profoundly impacted his life, filling it with a sense of purpose and guiding him with pure and noble ideals.

These ideals shaped his choices, especially when he reached the age of marriage. For Abdullah, the key qualities of a potential spouse are Taqwa (God-Consciousness), Akhlaq (Character), and sharing the same life mission.

He often said, "We must raise a generation of good citizens who can lead society guided by ethical principles and values, ultimately seeking the pleasure of the Almighty."

His sincerity was evident in every word.

It seems that Allah heard his prayers, for He blessed Abdullah with a life partner who embodied the purity and virtue he had always desired.

This was a sign of Allah's eternal peace to Abdullah in the Hereafter.

I often heard him express his gratitude for this blessing. "May Allah's favours continue in such a way!" he would say.

Both Abdullah and his wife deeply understood the true purpose of life.

They were clear and determined that their ultimate goal was to earn Allah's pleasure.

This belief was the cornerstone of their future together and was evident in every aspect of their daily lives.

They never missed an opportunity to make *dua* (supplication) in every prayer, especially concerning their children.

Unlike many parents who only start thinking about a child's name after birth, Abdullah and his wife differ.

They planned every detail, even before their child was born. They envisioned the qualities and virtues they hoped their future children would embody.

Their greatest desire was to raise a child, a "Siddique," who could bring Allah's guidance back to life on Earth.

When their son was born seven days later, they officially named him "Siddique" and celebrated this beautiful beginning.

Abdullah later shared with me the details of his heartfelt prayer during his long *Sajada* while his wife was in labour.

His sincere and devotional words remain etched in my memory.

They are potent reminders to all parents and guiding principles that every parent should embrace.

-

Ya Allah!

Today, our society is moving away from Your guidance. This must change, and we need people to bring that change.

Ya Allah!

Let individuals of such character be born from my descendants!

Let them tirelessly work to establish Your guidance in society.

Let them be capable of reviving the efforts of Your righteous servants who have restored Your guidance throughout history.

Grant me the ability to guide my children as a devoted father!

Ya Allah!

In just a few moments, you will grant me a precious gift.

Allow us to nurture it with the purpose for which You created it!

Make my wife the best partner to fulfil this responsibility perfectly!

Bless her with steadfast faith, noble virtues, and good health!

On the Day of Judgment, join us with the best parents who have received Your favour!

Accept and bless the humble supplication of this weak servant of Yours!

Ameen.

Abdullah's prayer was sincere and from the heart, and it seems Allah listened to his supplications.

The life of Siddique is a testament to that!

Abdullah and his wife were fully aware of the greatness of parenting.

They firmly believed that every child enters this world carrying a bundle of divine blessings—an innate awareness of their Creator, a spark of intelligence, the freedom to choose, a wellspring of desires, and untapped potential.

Hence, the role of parenting, then, is not merely to raise a child but to nurture these gifts with wisdom and care. It reminds them of their Creator and cultivates a deep sense of God-consciousness within their hearts.

Parents must provide an education that empowers them to make meaningful contributions to the world, guides them in making wise and ethical choices, and helps them channel their desires towards noble goals and pure motivations.

Moreover, parents must help their children uncover their hidden potential and inspire them to design their lives with purpose and meaning, aligned with a more excellent vision of goodness and service.

The Qur'an stands above all literature in the history of the world. It is the word of Allah, the Savior of humanity. Its recitation is soothing to the ears and calming to the soul.

When my sister, Fatima, discovered she was pregnant, she prioritised spending more time reciting, listening to, and studying the Qur'an.

She paid close attention to maintaining and protecting her senses, understanding that Taqwa (God-consciousness) is the only means of earning honour with Allah. She tried to improve her Taqwa by fasting, saluting the Prophet, and giving charity.

From the earliest days of Siddique's life, both Abdullah and his wife were committed to securing Allah's love and mercy for him.

After each prayer, they dedicated a special moment to Siddique.

They would speak to Allah about the qualities they hoped Siddique would develop.

Along with the nourishment of milk, they poured their love and blessings into him.

With every feeding, they prayed, "Ya Allah! Grant him an

understanding of Your religion and comprehensive knowledge of the Qur'an!"

They knew the common lullabies and their meanings but didn't believe these would help develop their child's soul with virtuous qualities.

Therefore, Fatima composed her songs centred on monotheism and spiritual yearning, even though she wasn't exceptionally skilled in songwriting or singing!

The first word Siddique uttered was "Allah." When they heard it, both parents were overjoyed.

Even though Siddique didn't understand its meaning at that young age, they took it as a declaration of the guiding principle for his future life.

As Siddique grew older and reached the age where he could understand what he saw and heard, his parents became very cautious about his upbringing.

They tried to protect Siddique's five senses from negative influences, shielding his eyes and ears from anything that could attract unhealthy attention.

This was no easy task in a time when television and movies dominated.

They were also very mindful of inappropriate conversations among children.

Some people viewed their efforts as unnecessary and advised them that protecting a child's environment this way was practically impossible.

They argued that children should be exposed to good and bad things or would eventually learn everything independently, regardless of their parent's actions.

Others would dismiss the matter, believing that the children would turn out fine as adults if Allah would.

Those who thought this way could never understand the ideals and responsibility Abdullah and his wife felt toward their child.

They couldn't see the potential long-term benefits of their efforts.

Many people don't understand that children are like clay, ready to be shaped into whatever mould we desire.

And many are not prepared to invest the time and energy required for this noble task.

Bedtime storytelling was one of Abdullah and his wife's most effective methods of shaping Siddique's character.

They avoided popular children's stories that often featured lying, cheating, jealousy, and pride.

Instead, they adapted these stories to focus on themes of heaven, monotheism, and virtues.

They also created original stories in which Siddique himself was the hero.

-

Once upon a time, there was a lovely little village. On the edge of this village, a boy lived with his parents in a small house.

One day, the boy's mother, Umma, had to go out for something important. She was gone for a long time, and the boy felt hungry.

He wasn't used to going out alone without his mother, so he stayed inside, unsure what to do.

But as his hunger grew, he decided to go to his uncle's house, also in the village.

Though he had never wandered outside alone, he decided to be brave and step out, saying "Bismillah" (In Allah's name).

As he was walking, he saw an old woman making hot, crispy cookies in a small hut near his house.

The boy was so hungry that he wanted to take one of the cookies from her plate and run away.

But then, he remembered his mother's words that taking things that are not yours is wrong. So, he decided not to do it, but he still felt sad and hungry.

The boy noticed that the old woman was working very hard. Feeling sorry for her, he wanted to help.

He picked up some sticks and pieces of firewood and took them to her.

The old woman was very happy to see the boy's kindness.

She smiled and prayed to Allah to give him a bright future. To thank him, she gave him some cookies as a gift.

The boy thanked the old woman and ran joyfully back home with a big smile on his face.

-

Once upon a time, a kind and handsome boy named Siddique lived in a small village. Everyone knew him as a good boy.

One day, after school, Siddique was walking home. On his way, he heard some boys shouting.

Siddique, who didn't like to waste time with silly games, decided to walk quietly past them.

But suddenly, he heard a puppy crying and stopped right away. He saw a small puppy stuck in a drain nearby, unable to climb.

Instead of helping the poor puppy, the boys threw stones at it and teased it. Siddique felt very sad seeing this.

Siddique quickly told the boys that what they were doing was wrong.

He shouted, "Allah does not like it when people are cruel to animals!" Hearing his words, the boys felt ashamed and slowly left the place.

Then, Siddique took a piece of rope with him and gently helped the puppy climb out of the drain.

The puppy wagged its tail as if to thank you and happily ran into the forest.

-

One day, Siddique played on a swing tied to a big mango tree in his backyard with his friends.

The tree had ripe mangoes hanging from it, and some of the boys couldn't resist wanting to pick them.

Before they started playing, Siddique told everyone, "After we finish playing, I will give you some mangoes. But please, don't throw stones at the mango tree."

However, one naughty boy didn't listen. He picked up a stone and threw it at the tree.

But he missed, and the stone flew far away and hit the umbrella of a man walking by on the path.

The man became very angry and shouted. When they heard him, all the boys ran away, except Siddique.

The man came over, grabbed Siddique's hand, and shook him roughly. He threatened to punish him.

But Siddique stood there calmly, without any fear or worry. Surprised to see Siddique so calm, the man asked why he wasn't scared.

"Uncle, my friend threw the stone, but he got scared and ran away. He didn't mean to hit you," Siddique replied calmly. "Please forgive us."

Hearing Siddique's honest and kind words, the man's anger faded, and he smiled.

He reached into his bag, took out some sweets, gave them to Siddique, and gently kissed him on the forehead.

-

By weaving such stories, Abdullah and his wife instilled their values into Siddique's heart and mind.

As he grew older and could understand more, they narrated the significant historical events in a storytelling style suited for his age.

Even if Siddique fell asleep before the end of a story, its impact would still leave a deep impression on his mind and soul. His life is a testament to their wise approach.

I interrupted him and said ...

Uncle, as far as I know, Brother Siddique is not the only child in his family. He has some siblings—both brothers and sisters.

In families with multiple children, it is common for parents to struggle with maintaining equality among them.

This often leads to feelings of jealousy or competition, which can hinder the development of genuine love and affection between siblings.

The challenge becomes even more complicated when the age gap between the children is very small, as their needs and interests overlap more, making conflicts more likely.

I am currently facing this very problem myself. Balancing the attention, love, and care among my children without anyone feeling left out or less loved is proving to be quite a challenge.

It requires wisdom, patience, and understanding, but it's easier said than done.

But how did Abdullah achieve this balance in his family remarkably well?

--

Fatima was overjoyed when the doctor confirmed her pregnancy again.

The news filled her heart with excitement and apprehension.

Siddique was not even two years old then, and managing a toddler and a newborn seemed daunting.

But she and Abdullah saw it differently—it was a precious blessing from Allah, a divine gift meant to be cherished.

For them, the birth of a child was always a matter of Allah's will.

It is He who decides when and to whom a child is given. With this belief firmly rooted in their hearts, Siddique's parents always included a special plea in their prayers:

"Ya Allah! Grant us the best people you will give the world this century!"

With this faith, they began making all the necessary preparations for the arrival of their second child.

They understood this was about readying the home with baby clothes and a crib and preparing Siddique's young mind to welcome his new sibling warmly.

They often spoke to Siddique about the coming baby, using simple stories and examples he could understand.

They told him how exciting it would be to have a younger brother or sister and how he would be a loving elder sibling.

Slowly, Siddique's curiosity and excitement grew. He often asked his mother when he could meet his new brother or sister, eagerly waiting for the day.

Months passed, and soon enough, the day arrived. Fatima gave birth to a healthy second child.

They accepted the newborn with immense joy and gratitude. But as they brought the baby home, well-meaning neighbours and relatives began to share their concerns.

"Don't let Siddique see the baby too soon," some suggested. "He might get jealous or even hurt the baby," others warned.

However, they didn't know how carefully Siddique's mind and heart had been prepared to welcome the new family member.

Fatima, holding the baby close, went straight to Siddique. She showered him with kisses and smiles and gently said,

"I have brought you a special present." She carefully placed the newborn in Siddique's little arms and whispered, "You must take care of it very kindly."

Siddique looked at the tiny baby in his lap with wide eyes. His surprise soon turned into a gentle curiosity.

He slowly reached out, softly touching the baby's head, nose, ears, eyes, and tiny hands.

Then, a smile slowly spread across his face. Leaning forward, he placed a delicate kiss on the baby's belly.

Witnessing this tender moment, Siddique's parents were filled with indescribable joy.

Others, who had been so worried about Siddique's reaction, were pleasantly surprised.

Abdullah, moved by the sight, gathered his children in his arms and raised a heartfelt prayer to Allah, asking for His blessings for their future.

He prayed for their hearts to be filled with love and affection for each other, hoping that they would always grow up in harmony and unity.

From that day on, Siddique's parents dedicated themselves to nurturing that bond between their children.

With patience, wisdom, and love, they ensured that all their children grew up with a strong sense of affection, kindness, and understanding for each other.

--

Many people think instilling a sense of competition in children is an excellent way to boost their performance. But there is a fine line between healthy competition and the dangerous feeling of jealousy.

Parents often push their children to outperform others, hoping this sense of competition will drive them to succeed.

However, they don't realise that doing so can slowly erode the beautiful qualities of love, kindness, and the desire to help others.

Siddique's parents took a different approach.

They wanted to see their children excel, but they did not believe in pushing them to compete against one another.

Instead, they used gentle and thoughtful strategies to improve their children's performance in ways that nurtured the values they held dear.

These methods aligned with the purpose they were created—to build strong, loving, and compassionate individuals.

Rather than raising rivalry, Siddique's parents taught their children the importance of helping one another and living harmoniously.

They explained that true success lies in competing and lifting one another.

They often reminded their children that Allah's love was the key to entering Jannah (Heaven), where they would find everything their hearts desired.

This teaching instilled in them a deep desire to earn Allah's favour through good deeds, love, and kindness.

From a young age, Siddique and his siblings were taught that the path to Jannah was paved with good behaviour and pure intentions.

Their parents used this desire to shape their actions, guiding them towards good things and avoiding harmful behaviours.

For example, they introduced simple Duas (supplications) into their daily routines.

Instead of forcing the children to memorise these prayers, they recited them aloud during everyday activities—when waking up, before eating, or before sleeping—so they would naturally learn them over time.

The parents also made these lessons engaging.

They would tell the children that when they do good deeds or say their Duas, Allah is happy upon them and sends angels to protect them.

This simple but profound statement captivated the children's imaginations, making them eager to do things that would make Allah happy.

These teachings were especially useful when small quarrels arose between Siddique and his siblings over trivial matters.

Like any other children, they would occasionally fight over toys or misunderstandings. But their parents' deep-seated desire for Jannah, which they had nurtured in their hearts, often helped to resolve these disputes quickly.

The children would remember that being kind and forgiving, especially with siblings, could bring them closer to Allah's love and, ultimately, to Jannah.

In this way, Siddique's parents managed to create a nurturing environment where the children thrived, not through competition or jealousy but through love, support, and a shared spiritual goal.

It was exciting. Then I asked...

"Uncle!"

"Many parents face a common challenge when raising their children. I've seen many families where parents are very strict about how they want their children to behave."

"These children often act like angels at home, always following the rules."

"But outside the house, the story can be quite different. The children's behaviour in public may not always match how they act at home."

"So, how did Abdullah handle this situation? "How did he ensure that his children behaved well at home and outside?"

--

Many parents often find their children to be quite a handful at home.

They sometimes send their kids out to play to give themselves a break, thinking it's a great solution. But they don't always pay much attention to where the children go or who they play with.

Abdullah and his wife were different. They cared deeply about who their child, Siddique, spent time with.

They knew children who grew up surrounded by television and movies might develop bad habits, so they carefully ensured Siddique played with the right friends.

Abdullah and his wife stayed very close to the parents of Siddique's friends.

They shared their values and tried to guide the other parents on how to raise their children.

They preferred that Siddique and his friends play at home so they could monitor their behaviour.

They were kind to all the children who came over and told them good stories. They even set up little games to teach them positive traits.

Every night before bed, Abdullah and his wife discussed Siddique's day in a fun and engaging way.

They praised the good things he did and gently corrected any mistakes he made.

Another approach Abdullah used was to form close friendships with other families with children around Siddique's age.

They held regular family meetings, discussing their experiences and sharing advice on raising children.

This allowed Siddique to befriend other kids with similar values.

When Siddique was four years old, something showed the results of Abdullah and his wife's efforts.

-

One day, Siddique went to play with his neighbours but soon came running back to his mother, crying. Other children followed him, and they all looked upset.

Siddique was crying because one of his neighbour's friends had taken his toy car. The other kids were making the situation sound even worse.

Umm, Siddique's mother, hugged him and whispered comforting words while kissing him on the forehead.

As soon as Siddique felt his mother's love, his tears started to fade, much to the other children's surprise.

Suddenly, Siddique's face brightened up. He called, "Janna! Janna!" and returned to the neighbour's house.

Not understanding what was happening, the other children shouted, "Janna! Janna!" and followed him.

When Siddique reached the neighbour's house, he told the friend who had taken his car, "You can keep the car. I will get more beautiful and bigger cars than that." Then he went home.

The friend, puzzled and curious, came out of his house and chased after Siddique and the others.

They all wanted to know how Siddique could get those bigger cars and where they would come from.

Siddique smiled big, saying, "My Ummah said that Allah will give me more beautiful and bigger cars in Jannah because I gave you my car."

The other children were amazed and asked, "What's Jannah? Where is it?" They were eager to understand.

Siddique then asked everyone to sit down and took his mother's hand. He wanted her to explain Jannah to his friends.

When Umm Siddique saw how her son shared his faith, she was filled with joy and happiness.

She praised Allah for guiding Siddique to be so thoughtful and kind.

--

Abdullah and his wife understood that the first five years of a child's life were the most important for shaping their mind and character.

They were committed to ensuring that their son, Siddique, would grow up surrounded by good thoughts, higher ideas, and righteous people.

Since Siddique was just a few months old, he has been blessed to participate in Islamic events. His mother, Umm Siddique, would carry him along wherever she went.

She believed the positive environment would still leave a mark on his soul even if he were too young to understand the discussions and prayers.

When Siddique turned four, Abdullah ensured that Siddique attended Islamic gatherings with him.

Abdullah never missed an opportunity to bring his son to these events, even if some thought it wasn't worth it for such a young child. But Abdullah saw things differently.

He believed that even though Siddique might not grasp the discussions or ideas shared at the gatherings, he needed to become familiar with the sound of kind words, wise thoughts, and the company of good people.

Abdullah also believed that taking Siddique to these gatherings allowed him to be blessed by Allah and receive the prayers of the angels, which surrounded good events.

He was friends with many respected men in their town and made it a point to introduce Siddique to them.

He was sure these meetings with wise and good-hearted men would positively shape his son's personality.

-

One Friday afternoon, Abdullah held young Siddique's hand as they made their way to a small gathering at the mosque.

Siddique, just four years old, bounced along happily, not fully understanding where they were going but excited to spend time with his father.

As they entered the mosque, the room was filled with the gentle hum of men greeting one another, exchanging pleasantries, and preparing for the day's discussion.

Abdullah led Siddique to a quiet corner where they could sit, and he greeted several familiar faces.

The elders noticed Siddique smiling warmly at the young boy, one by one.

Some of the men gave Abdullah curious glances, wondering why he would bring such a young child to a discussion Siddique clearly wouldn't understand.

One of Abdullah's friends, a kind man named Ahmed, leaned over and whispered, "Isn't he a little too young for this, Abdullah? Surely, he won't remember much."

Abdullah smiled gently. "Perhaps not, but that's not why I bring him. He may not understand the words, but he'll feel the blessings.

He'll hear the kind words and be surrounded by goodness. In time, this atmosphere will shape him."

As the gathering began, wise men shared stories of the Prophet (PBUH), lessons on patience, and reminders of Allah's mercy.

Though too young to follow the conversation, Siddique listened intently to the soothing tones and watched the men speak with kindness and wisdom.

His little eyes darted from speaker to speaker, absorbing the warmth in the room.

At one point, an elderly man across from them caught Siddique's gaze and smiled.

He raised his hands in prayer, and Abdullah, noticing this, whispered to Siddique, "You see, my son, these are good men.

They pray for others, for our community, and even for you. Allah's blessings are with those who gather in goodness."

After such gatherings ended, Abdullah used to take Siddique around to meet the elders.

"This is my son, Siddique," he said, introducing him to each man.

The elders greeted Siddique warmly, their hands resting gently on his head as they offered prayers and blessings.

One man, known for his wisdom, knelt to Siddique's level and said, "May Allah make you a beacon of knowledge and goodness."

Though Siddique was too young to understand what was being said fully, he felt the love and care in the room.

He didn't yet know the meaning of the words, but the kindness imprinted his heart.

-

As the years passed, these gatherings became a regular part of Siddique's life.

Each time he attended, he felt a little more connected to the wisdom shared, and the blessings spoken over him shaped his character.

By the time he was old enough to understand the discussions, he had already developed a love for the company of good people and the pursuit of wisdom.

Abdullah's simple act of bringing his young son to these gatherings had, over time, instilled in Siddique a deep sense of purpose, community, and faith.

The seeds of goodness sown in those early years blossomed into a life guided by wisdom, humility, and kindness.

--

Abdullah and his wife didn't stop there. They made other very fruitful efforts.

They were particularly strict about honesty.

They did not lie, not even small lies, and they made sure not to lie to Siddique.

They wanted to set an example for him. Siddique learned to always stick to the truth, whether he fully understood it.

Sometimes, the situation might have tempted them to tell a small lie or make an excuse, but they consistently avoided it.

This taught Siddique to be truthful and honest, even when difficult.

-

Abdullah and his wife sat Siddique at the dinner table one beautiful evening.

It was time for their evening meal, but more importantly, it was a moment for the family to gather and talk.

Fatima, Fatima, had prepared a simple but delicious dinner.

As they began to eat, Siddique's eyes sparkled with curiosity. "Umma, did you make the dessert tonight?"

Fatima hesitated for a moment. She had bought the dessert from a local bakery because she was too tired to bake it herself.

She knew it would be easy to say she made it, but she chose to be honest instead.

"No, Siddique," she said with a gentle smile. "I didn't make it. We bought it from the bakery today."

Siddique looked surprised but nodded.

Abdullah, who had been quietly observing, added, "It's important to always tell the truth, even about small things.

Even if we think it's easier to say something else, honesty helps us build trust and respect."

The conversation reminded Siddique of a lesson he had learned earlier.

One day, Siddique accidentally broke a classmate's toy at school.

He was tempted to say it was an accident he didn't cause, but he remembered his parents' example.

When his teacher asked about the toy, Siddique admitted to his mistake.

"I'm sorry, I broke the toy," he confessed.

His teacher praised him for his honesty, and his classmates respected him for being truthful.

One day, while grocery shopping, a cashier accidentally gave Abdullah an extra change.

Abdullah noticed the mistake but quietly returned the money to the cashier, explaining the error.

Watching the entire interaction, Siddique felt a surge of pride and admiration for his parents.

"Umma, Dad, why did you return the extra money?" Siddique asked later.

"Because it's the right thing to do,"

Abdullah explained. "Even if no one else noticed, we must be honest and fair in all our actions. It's important to do what's right, even when difficult."

Siddique understood. He realised his parents taught him to be honest and live with integrity.

-

As Siddique grew older, the lessons he learned from his parents became deeply ingrained.

He faced challenges and temptations, but the foundation of honesty and integrity that Abdullah and Fatima had built in him guided him through each situation.

He learned that truthfulness wasn't just a rule to follow but a way of life that shaped his character and interactions with others.

In every choice he made, Siddique carried forward the values instilled in him by his parents, knowing that honesty was not merely a principle but a cornerstone of his identity and relationships.

--

Abdullah and Fatima were also careful not to embarrass Siddique in front of others by pointing out his faults.

They didn't rush to punish or scold him for every little mistake. Instead, they guided him gently with kind words at the right moments.

Some parents would beat their children for minor mistakes, while others, following a more modern approach, would let their children behave however they wanted.

But Siddique's parents chose a middle path.

They believed that a light tap could sometimes serve as a tool to discipline their child, but they never used it in a way that caused pain or fear.

Through this balanced approach, Siddique learned valuable lessons about right and wrong.

-

Siddique and his parents enjoyed a family picnic at the local park one Saturday afternoon.

Siddique was excitedly playing with his friends, running around and laughing.

Amidst the fun, he accidentally knocked over a picnic basket, spilling its contents all over the grass.

Abdullah and Fatima observed the incident from a distance. Although some food was ruined, they handled the situation calmly.

Instead of reacting with anger or embarrassment, they waited for a quiet moment to talk to Siddique.

As the picnic continued, Siddique joined his parents. He could see their concern and knew that he had done something wrong.

Abdullah gently touched Siddique's shoulder and said, "Siddique, accidents happen, but we must be more careful. Let's clean up the mess together."

Siddique nodded, feeling a mix of embarrassment and relief.

Fatima handed him a cloth, and they tidied the picnic area together.

While they worked, Abdullah spoke softly, "It's important to be mindful of our surroundings and respectful of the things we have. If you make a mistake, it's okay, but we should always try to fix it and learn from it."

As they cleaned up, Siddique's friends came over to help. He appreciated their support and felt reassured by his parents' gentle guidance.

Abdullah and Fatima's approach allowed Siddique to learn from his mistake without feeling ashamed or punished harshly.

-

As Siddique grew, Abdullah and Fatima continued to support him with this balanced approach.

They offered gentle corrections when needed and encouraged positive behaviour through understanding and kindness.

Siddique learned to value his parents' lessons, understanding that discipline was about guiding him to make better choices rather than instilling fear.

--

Like most children, Siddique often asked for things when he saw something he liked.

For many parents, this can be a difficult situation. Some would give in to their child's demands with a grumble, while others would promise to buy it later, only to forget.

This only teaches children to be deceitful.

Abdullah and his wife handled these situations differently. If they could afford it, they would happily fulfil Siddique's wishes.

They would explain why they couldn't buy it and kindly refuse if they couldn't.

This honest approach built deep trust and respect in Siddique's heart for his parents.

-

Abdullah, Fatima, and Siddique went to the bustling town market one Friday afternoon.

As they wandered through the stalls, Siddique's eyes widened with excitement when he saw a bright red kite adorned with colourful patterns.

"Umma, can we buy that kite?" Siddique asked eagerly, pointing to the stall where the kite was displayed.

Abdullah and Fatima glanced at each other. They had set a budget for their outing, and buying the kite meant spending more than planned.

Abdullah knelt to Siddique's level and said gently, "I see you like that kite, Siddique. It looks wonderful. But right now, we have to stick to our budget for today. We can't buy it this time, but maybe next time we come to the market, we can see if it's still available."

Siddique's face fell slightly, but he appreciated his dad's honesty. "Oh, okay," he said, clearly disappointed.

Fatima added, "Sometimes, we have to make choices and prioritise what we need most. But I promise, we'll think about getting one for you when we have a special occasion or if we can afford it."

Later that day, as they were leaving the market, Siddique spotted a small toy he had been eyeing for a while.

This time, Abdullah and Fatima saw that Siddique had shown restraint and understood the need for patience.

Abdullah said as they approached the toy stall, "Siddique, we have a little extra left in our budget today. If you want this toy, we can buy it. But remember, it's important to consider our choices and ensure we get things we need or will enjoy."

Siddique thought momentarily and smiled, "I'd like it, Dad." Then, his sister Amira smiled at his father.

They bought two small toys, and the children were thrilled.

As they walked home, he looked up at his parents with gratitude and said, "Thank you for being honest with me and letting me choose."

-

Over time, Siddique learned that his parents' honest approach was more than just saying no or delaying gratification.

It was about teaching him the value of patience, budgeting, and making informed choices.

He grew to appreciate their transparency, fostering a deep trust and respect for them.

He understood that his parents' decisions were based on their commitment to his well-being, and this honesty became a cornerstone of their relationship.

--

Abdullah and his wife also taught Siddique about respect. Speaking poorly of others was not tolerated in their home.

They wanted to protect Siddique from an environment where people gossiped or criticised others. They also tried to instil in him a deep respect for elders.

Whenever they had guests, they would introduce them to Siddique beforehand, helping him build a good impression of them.

Likewise, when they visited others, they spoke positively about the people they were visiting.

They always encouraged Siddique to think well of others.

When they saw someone doing something wrong, they didn't criticise them in front of Siddique. Instead, they taught him to feel compassion for them.

This was their way of instilling the spirit of Da'wa or inviting others to good in Siddique's heart.

-

One evening, as the family was walking home from the local park, they noticed a young man arguing loudly with a shopkeeper.

The argument escalated, and the young man's harsh words and behaviour were upsetting.

Siddique, who was only six then, looked concerned and confused.

He turned to his parents and asked, "Why is that man shouting? Is he being mean?"

Instead of responding with criticism or judgment, Abdullah and Fatima took a gentle approach.

They walked with Siddique further down the path and found a quiet spot to talk.

Abdullah began, "Sometimes, people get upset and act in ways that aren't the best. We don't know what's going on in their lives or what challenges they might be facing."

Fatima added, "It's important to remember that everyone has their struggles. Instead of being angry or judgmental, we should try to feel compassion for them. They might need help or understanding, even if they don't know how to ask for it."

Siddique listened carefully, his eyes reflecting a mixture of curiosity and concern.

"So, we shouldn't be mean to them even if they're mean to others?"

"That's right," Abdullah said with a smile.

"We should always aim to be kind and understanding. If we can, we should try to help others and show them a better way through our actions."

Fatima continued, "This is also part of Da'wa, inviting others to do good. By showing compassion and understanding, we can help people see a better path and inspire them to make positive changes."

Siddique nodded thoughtfully.

-

Through these experiences, Abdullah and Fatima successfully instilled the spirit of Da'wa in Siddique's heart.

He learned that showing kindness and understanding was a powerful way to influence others positively and that everyone deserved compassion, especially when they were struggling.

--

One of Abdullah's family's most beautiful traditions was eating together. Meals weren't just about food; they were a time for teaching manners, enhancing closeness, and strengthening their bond as a family.

These moments often led to deep and meaningful conversations, especially at dinner.

Abdullah and his wife also believed in the importance of order and cleanliness. They taught Siddique that things are more beautiful and appealing when tidy and organised.

They knew that if good habits were not formed early, correcting them later would be much more difficult.

Through all these thoughtful and loving efforts, Abdullah and his wife built a strong foundation for Siddique's future, ensuring he grew up with good values, a strong character, and a heart full of faith.

--

When Siddique was a young boy, his parents, Abdullah and Umm Siddique, were very particular about teaching him how to behave in different situations.

They knew that good manners were the foundation of a strong character, so they took the time to explain things to him but maturely.

For instance, they taught him how to behave when visiting other people's houses.

"Siddique," his mother would say gently, "when we go to someone else's home, we must respect their space. We should not touch things without permission and must always be polite."

She explained that it was important to be careful with other people's belongings and to treat their home with the same care he would show in his own. His father would add,

"If you see something you like, don't just grab it. Ask first. This shows respect."

At home, Siddique also learned the importance of sharing. His parents taught him how to share his toys with the children who came to visit.

"When your friends come over," his father would say, "make sure everyone feels included. Share your toys and take turns. This way, everyone has fun, and no one feels left out."

They taught him how to be generous and kind while playing with other kids, making him understand that sharing would bring happiness to himself and others.

They would create scenarios, role-play different situations, and praise him when he shared nicely with his friends.

While many children struggled to grasp these lessons, Siddique's parents approached them with patience and clarity.

They never forced children but always explained the reasons behind their advice.

Slowly but surely, Siddique began to understand the value of these lessons.

He saw that respecting others' homes and sharing his toys made his friends happier and made him feel good.

Siddique's parents also taught him the value of compassion, especially toward those less fortunate.

Unlike many people who turned away beggars at their doorstep or treated them with annoyance, Abdullah and Umm Siddique saw these moments as opportunities for teaching.

"When someone asks for help," his mother would explain, "it's a chance to be kind. Even a small act of kindness can mean a lot to someone in need."

For Siddique, the arrival of a poor person at their door was a moment of excitement, not annoyance.

-

There was a gentle knock on the door. Siddique, a curious little boy, quickly ran to see who it was.

When he opened the door, he saw a woman standing there. She looked tired and worn out, and next to her stood a boy.

The boy's shirt was torn, and his feet were bare, clinging to his mother's saree. Siddique could tell right away that they were poor and needed help.

Without a second thought, Siddique turned around and hurried back into the house. He knew exactly what he wanted to do.

He went straight to his small piggy bank, where he kept his saved coins and carefully counted out some change.

His heart felt light and happy as he scooped up the coins and returned to the door.

With a big smile on his face, Siddique handed the coins to the woman.

"Here, Aunty, please take this," he chirped.

The woman looked at Siddique with kind eyes and gratefully accepted the money.

She thanked him softly and turned to leave. The boy walked slowly by her side, smiling shyly at Siddique.

Siddique stood at the door, watching them as they began to walk away.

His eyes were fixed on the child, who looked back at him with a gentle smile.

He seemed so small and fragile, and a thought crossed Siddique's mind.

He quickly approached them and asked, "Don't you have a dad?"

The little boy shook his head, saying, 'No. ' Siddique's heart sank slightly, and his face showed worry.

He thought momentarily, then said, "Wait here for just a minute!"

He darted back into the house, his little feet pattering on the floor.

Inside, Siddique went to his closet and pulled out a new shirt. It was his favourite—a beautiful, colourful outfit his father had recently bought for a big day. But Siddique didn't think twice.

He wanted to help the boy, so he returned and handed the shirt to the woman.

"Please, let her wear this," he said, his eyes filled with hope.

The woman looked at the shirt and gasped.

"Oh no, dear child," she said, shaking her head. "This is too much. This shirt is new, and it looks exceptional."

But Siddique insisted, "No, no, please take it.

He needs it more than I do." He was firm and kept urging the woman until she finally gave in.

With a grateful smile and tears in her eyes, the woman took the shirt and gently dressed the little boy.

The child's eyes sparkled with happiness as he twirled in his new clothes. Siddique's face lit up with joy as he watched the little boy.

Siddique's mother, Umm Siddique, was watching everything inside the house. She had seen her son's kindness, and her eyes welled up with tears of joy.

She was so proud of him that her heart felt glowing. "SubhanAllah," she whispered, praising Allah for blessing her with such a compassionate son.

"This moment," she thought, "is worth more than a thousand new clothes."

Her heart swelled with happiness, knowing her son had chosen to give away something precious to bring joy to someone in need.

She knew Siddique's kindness was a big lesson in generosity that would stay with him forever.

--

Over time, Siddique became known in his neighbourhood for his good manners and kind heart.

His parents' teachings were bearing fruit.

His friends admired him, and adults often remarked on how well-behaved and considerate he was for his age.

He had learned how to treat others respectfully and kindly, whether they were friends, visitors, or strangers in need.

Siddique's understanding and behaviour were not just lessons taught; they resulted from a loving environment where his parents practised what they preached.

Through daily examples and consistent guidance, they nurtured a young boy who was polite, respectful, compassionate, and eager to help others. They knew that was the foundation for a good life.

One person's most important character trait is facing problems and challenges with courage and wisdom.

Abdullah, a thoughtful father, clearly envisioned his children's future.

He believed children should grow up to be good people capable of handling life's difficulties with strength and grace.

In line with this aspiration, Abdullah carefully considered the personality traits his children would need to succeed and fulfil their purpose outstandingly.

He knew that solid character would be essential to carry out their missions with excellence, whatever they might be.

Abdullah took the time to observe the children closely. He noticed their actions, behaviours, and natural inclinations.

From these observations, he identified the qualities already present in them.

These were the building blocks of a strong character, and

Abdullah was proud to see them already taking root in his children.

But Abdullah also knew that every child, no matter how naturally talented, has areas where they need to grow.

He was mindful of the skills and strengths that still needed attention and cultivation.

Abdullah understood that these qualities would not develop overnight. They would require time, guidance, and consistent effort.

Abdullah set out to nurture these traits in children with a loving but firm hand.

He encouraged them to take on small challenges, solve problems independently, and learn from their mistakes.

Through these experiences, he knew children would develop the resilience, confidence, and decision-making skills crucial for their growth.

Through careful nurturing, Abdullah hoped to shape Siddique and his siblings to approach life's problems thoughtfully and bravely rather than reacting to them.

He aimed to help them become wise leaders who stand firm in principles and bring positive change to the community and the world.

--

Communication skills play a significant role in shaping a person's personality.

Understanding this, Abdullah and his wife focused on developing their children's language abilities from an early age.

They believed communicating clearly and confidently would be essential for Siddique's future.

Since Siddique could speak, Fatima has been attentive to how he pronounced letters and words.

Abdullah patiently taught him how to say each sound correctly, ensuring that Siddique's speech was clear and precise.

As Siddique grew older, Abdullah encouraged him to expand his vocabulary.

He would engage Siddique in conversations about various topics, prompting him to use new words.

Abdullah often took Siddique to places like parks, museums, and even local markets to make learning more exciting.

This allowed him to encounter new experiences and learn new words.

Abdullah also understood the importance of knowing multiple languages in today's world.

He tried to introduce Siddique to international languages, believing that being multilingual would help him interact confidently and fluently in any situation.

Whether learning simple greetings or phrases in different languages or listening to stories from other cultures, Siddique was given many opportunities to develop his communication skills in a fun and engaging way.

Abdullah often narrated stories of historical heroes to strengthen Siddique's heart and mind.

He would talk about the noble qualities of great achievers in a way that Siddique could easily understand.

He told tales of bravery, honesty, kindness, and perseverance.

Each story was more than just a tale—it was a lesson that Abdullah linked to Siddique's future.

He would explain why these qualities were essential and how they could help Siddique in his own life.

He enjoyed seeing Siddique's eyes light up with understanding and interest whenever he heard about these traits.

In addition to language and storytelling, Abdullah believed physical courage was just as necessary.

He gradually introduced Siddique to sports and games that could help build his bravery.

Simple games that involved some risk, like climbing or racing, were regular parts of their activities.

Abdullah would offer small prizes whenever Siddique participated and showed an effort to motivate him further.

These games were about winning and developing a fearless and resilient spirit.

Over time, Abdullah's efforts began to show.

Siddique became more confident in his communication, expressing his thoughts clearly and with a growing vocabulary.

He was also becoming braver and willing to face new challenges, whether in conversations or physical activities.

For Abdullah, watching his son grow in this way was incredibly rewarding.

He knew he was laying the foundation for a future in which Siddique would be well-equipped to handle whatever came his way—strong in mind and heart, ready to communicate, lead, and inspire.

Fatima would gently wake Siddique and his younger sisters every morning for their special Quranic memorisation session.

Despite their young age, the children had come to look forward to these moments, knowing they would begin with the shorter chapters of the Qur'an, which are manageable for their developing minds.

-

One morning, Fatima, Fatima settled down with Siddique beside her.

"Let's recite this chapter together," she said, pointing to the verses in the Qur'an. Still half-asleep and hesitant,

Siddique looked at the text with wide eyes.

But as the rhythmic flow of the recitation began, he slowly started to enjoy the process.

His tiny fingers traced the lines of text, and soon, he was reciting along, the hesitation fading away.

Whenever Siddique successfully memorised a new verse or

chapter, Abdullah and Fatima would come together to celebrate his achievement.

Their faces would light up with pride, and they would gather around, reciting the verses joyfully.

Hearing that noise, Amira, Siddique's younger sister, woke up and understood what was happening.

She joined eagerly in the recitations and memorisation sessions, sometimes even memorising chapters faster than Siddique.

Her quick progress often surprised and delighted their parents, adding an extra layer of joy to the family's daily routines.

The family's dedication to these morning sessions forged a strong bond as the years passed. Siddique and his sisters grew up with the verses of the Qur'an woven into their hearts.

The teachings of the Qur'an became a cherished part of their lives, guiding them through their days.

Every good deed and act of learning reminded them of the divine blessings and the enduring teachings they had learned from their parents.

--

Understanding the significance of the early years for brain development, Siddique's parents were deeply committed to making the most of this critical period.

They dedicated themselves to building a solid foundation for their children's ambitions.

This early focus on spiritual and intellectual growth prepared

Siddique and his sisters for their future roles and contributed to their overall well-being.

Thanks to the solid foundation during these formative years, they could maintain good health and protect themselves from common childhood illnesses.

--

Many people love to talk about science and share interesting facts they've learned.

They often say that the Qur'an mentioned these scientific facts 1400 years before scientists discovered them.

This makes people feel proud of the Qur'an and shows its greatness.

Abdullah, who was wise and thoughtful, had a different way of looking at this.

He believed that while connecting science with the Qur'an is excellent, it's important to remember that the Qur'an is much more special than any science.

When people use science to show how unique the Qur'an is, they sometimes make it seem like science is more important than the Qur'an. Abdullah thought that wasn't right.

Instead, Abdullah believed that learning about the Qur'an should come first.

He thought it was better to discuss the scientific facts from the Qur'an. Abdullah wanted his children to learn and appreciate the Qur'an deeply.

Abdullah also used what he learned from science to help explain how unique Allah's creations are.

He helped his children appreciate the Qur'an and its teachings more because they saw how it connected to everything around them.

Thanks to Abdullah's efforts, Siddique and his siblings developed a strong love for the Qur'an.

They learned to approach everything in life with the wisdom and guidance of the Qur'an.

They were grateful for Abdullah's approach and always remembered using the teachings of the Quran in all their adventures and discoveries.

Abdullah and Fatima understood the immense value of fostering strong relationships among their children.

They were deeply aware of the significance of blood relations, a divine blessing that is a guiding principle for maintaining family unity and, ultimately, strengthening the community.

From an early age, they instilled in their children the importance of caring for one another and sharing.

Whenever Abdullah brought home sweets, he often asked Siddique, or sometimes their eldest daughter, to divide and distribute them among all the siblings.

Though it was a challenging exercise, sharing soon became a cherished tradition in their home, even as the children grew older.

Over time, the children learned not only to share but also to sacrifice willingly.

On some occasions, they would give up their portions when a sibling earnestly requested more, finding joy in the act of selflessness.

-

One day, Abdullah walked into the house with a small box of sweets. His children, who had been playing in the yard, rushed to greet him, their eyes wide with excitement.

"Dad, what did you bring for us?" asked the youngest, barely able to contain his curiosity.

Abdullah smiled warmly, holding the box high. "Sweets for all of you," he said to his elder daughter, "Amira, I want you to share them with your siblings."

Amira hesitated for a moment. She had seen her older brother, Siddique, do it before, and it didn't seem that hard.

Yet, when the box was placed in her hands, she suddenly felt the weight of responsibility. Her four siblings stood around her, all eagerly awaiting their share.

With careful hands, Amira began to count the pieces. There were five sweets, just enough for each to have one. But as she handed out the last sweet, her hand came up empty.

For a moment, disappointment flashed in her eyes. She had been so excited to have a sweet of her own, but now it seemed she would go without.

Just as the thought crossed his mind, his older brother, Siddique, quietly handed his sweet back to Amira. "Here, you can have mine," he said with a smile. "I don't mind."

Amira blinked in surprise. "But... it's yours," she stammered.

"It's okay," Siddique replied. "I've had sweets before. It makes me happy to see you enjoy it."

Amira, touched by her brother's gesture, felt a warmth in her heart that was even sweeter than the treat she now held.

Without another word, she broke the sweet in half and handed part of it back to Siddique. They smiled at each other, their unspoken bond stronger than ever.

Abdullah, watching from a distance, felt immense pride in his chest. He glanced at his wife, Fatima, who stood by his side, smiling gently.

They had always taught their children the value of sharing, but today, they had witnessed the true beauty of selflessness.

--

Every Muslim has an essential duty to show through their words and actions.

One of the most vital tools Muslims must use to fulfil this duty is knowledge.

The Prophet Muhammad (PBUH) emphasised this importance by saying, "It is every Muslim's obligatory duty to seek and acquire knowledge."

Siddique's parents were deeply aware of this responsibility. They were determined to provide everything needed to prepare

Siddique and their other children for the mission they were born to undertake.

They knew reading was the first and most essential step in seeking knowledge. Reading opens the mind to new ideas, helps people understand the world, and builds a foundation for learning more complex concepts.

When Siddique was four, his parents started giving him disciplined reading lessons.

They encouraged him every day and made sure he spent time with books.

By the time he turned six, Siddique could read storybooks by himself! His vocabulary grew quickly, and he learned many new words and ideas daily.

It was clear that his mother, Umm Siddique, had worked hard to help him reach this stage.

At such a young age, when most children were busy playing, Siddique and his sister eagerly explored and absorbed new things into his curious mind.

By the age of eight, Siddique was already reading newspapers, biographies of historical figures, and books on natural science.

This wide range of reading helped him develop a deep understanding of different subjects and taught him to think critically.

He became skilled at interpreting information, understanding complex topics, and asking thoughtful questions.

Siddique's eagerness to learn also encouraged his parents to seek more knowledge.

They had to study hard to answer all of Siddique's challenging questions. This created a home environment where learning and seeking knowledge were highly valued.

Because of this, Siddique's younger siblings naturally picked up the habit of reading as well.

Over time, Siddique became a very skilled reader. He learned various techniques to make his reading more effective.

For example, he developed methods for scanning large books, memorising important ideas quickly, and comparing different types of writing on the same topic.

These experiences and practices helped Siddique gain special abilities that made him more effective in sharing knowledge and guidance with others.

Thanks to his parents' dedication and his love for learning, Siddique grew up with a strong foundation in knowledge.

He learned to use his skills to better himself and contribute positively to society.

His early reading habit and ability to know and understand quickly became powerful tools that helped him fulfil his duty as a Muslim, guiding others with wisdom and knowledge.

--

Charity or helping those in need does not come naturally to everyone. It can be challenging to give with a pure heart solely for the sake of Allah.

Understanding this, Abdullah and his wife were keen to develop this important quality in their children from a young age.

They believed that if the children learned the value of charity early on, it would become a natural part of their identity.

Whenever there was a chance to give or help someone, Abdullah would make a point to get the children excited about it.

He would share with them all the beautiful benefits of being charitable in this world and the Hereafter.

He would say, "Remember, everything we have is not ours; Allah gives it to us! So, when someone who does not have what they need comes to us, we should never turn them away or say no."

Through these discussions, Abdullah and his wife aimed to plant empathy and generosity in their children's hearts.

They taught them that giving without hesitation or refusal is essential when someone in need asks for help.

Abdullah and his wife were teachers not only in words but also in deeds. They always set a great example for their children.

There were times when they couldn't help someone due to their limitations, and in those moments, they would share their regret with their children, letting them see how much it mattered to them to help others.

This way, their children learned that charity is not just about giving money or things but about caring and feeling for others.

On all these occasions, Abdullah and his wife would remind their children of one very important lesson: "Never expect anything in return from anyone when you give to charity!"

They would explain that only Allah can genuinely reward their good deeds, and the blessings and rewards He has prepared in the Hereafter are far beyond what anyone in this world could give them in return.

They also taught their children to keep their charitable acts a secret.

They explained that doing so would bring them closer to Allah's love and grace and that Allah would prepare unlimited gifts for them in Jannah.

They told their children, "When you give quietly and secretly, it is like a special bond between you and Allah."

-

One day, like every other day, little Siddique came home from preschool, but there was something different about him.

His face was filled with joy, and his eyes sparkled with happiness. Fatima, his mother, noticed this right away. She tried to ask him why he was so happy.

"What's making you smile so much, Siddique?" she asked gently. But no matter how many times she asked, Siddique just kept smiling without saying a word.

The following day, something unexpected happened. Siddique told his mother that he didn't want to go to school.

This was unusual for him because he loved school and always went excitedly.

Fatima felt troubled. She had no idea why he didn't want to go to school, so she repeatedly asked him, "Why don't you want to go,

Siddique? Did something happen at school?"

But Siddique just stayed quiet. He didn't say a single word.

Worried, Fatima told her husband, Abdullah, about the situation. Abdullah thought carefully and felt something must have happened at school to make Siddique act this way.

"Maybe something unexpected happened," he said. He comforted his wife and advised her to recite the Awrad, a set of protective prayers, to calm their hearts. Then, he went to work.

That day, Siddique stayed home. He played happily by himself, singing songs he had learned at school.

He seemed cheerful and carefree, which confused Fatima even more. Her heart ached as she watched her son.

She wondered what could have made him so unwilling to go to school when he was usually so happy there. She cried quietly, feeling lost and unsure of what to do.

When Abdullah returned home in the evening, he went straight to Siddique.

He scooped him up, hugged him, and kissed him on the forehead. Abdullah's eyes filled with tears but were tears of joy, not sadness.

He then placed a small gift package in Siddique's hands.

Siddique's eyes widened with excitement as he opened the package. Inside was a beautiful new box of colours. Siddique's face lit up with happiness.

Siddique ran to his mother with a big smile, holding the colour box tightly.

"I can go to school tomorrow, Umma!" he shouted excitedly, hugging her.

Fatima was both happy and puzzled. She hugged Siddique back and asked kindly, "Why, Siddique? Why didn't you want to go to school today?"

Siddique showed her the colour box his father had given him. "Look, Umma! It's a new colour box!" he said, his face glowing joyfully.

Abdullah then explained what had happened.

"I went to meet Siddique's teacher today to find out what happened at school," he began.

"The teacher told me that Siddique is doing wonderfully at school. She also mentioned that he loves interacting with children, especially those less fortunate. He never says no when they ask for something and always shares whatever he has."

Abdullah continued, "Yesterday, a student asked for Siddique's colour box. Without thinking twice, Siddique gave it to him with a big smile. He didn't refuse.

The teacher was impressed by Siddique's kindness and willingness to help others."

Listening to this, Fatima felt a mix of emotions.

She was deeply touched but also worried, realising that Siddique didn't want to go to school today simply because he didn't have a colour box.

He had given away his only one. But now, seeing her son's happy face and knowing the reason behind his actions, she felt a wave of pride.

Furthermore, Siddique was hiding his charity, even from his parents.

When they asked him, Siddique looked at them with his innocent eyes and replied with a big smile.

"I wanted to get the full reward from Allah for doing a secret charity."

His words were simple but filled with wisdom far beyond his years.

Abdullah and Fatima looked at each other, their hearts swelling with joy.

Their little Siddique had shown such a big heart, the kind of heart that gives without expecting anything in return.

They were both grateful to Allah for blessing their son with such a generous spirit.

--

The consciousness of Da'wah, or inviting others to the path of rightness, is indeed a great blessing from Allah.

The desire to guide people's hearts towards Allah, the Creator and Sustainer of the world, is one of the highest and most noble feelings a person can have.

Only those blessed with this sense of responsibility and privilege can truly benefit human society and achieve real liberation for themselves and others.

Siddique's parents, Abdullah and Fatima, understood this deep truth very well.

They knew acquiring this feeling and passing it on to others was difficult. It requires careful nurturing and guidance from a very young age.

For this reason, they introduced certain unique teachings to their children, helping them understand the importance of Da'wah early on.

They encouraged their children to guide others to the right path whenever they noticed their mistakes or shortcomings.

"Whenever you see someone doing something wrong, invite them to do good and show them the right way," they would say.

When meeting non-Muslims, they taught their children a deep sense of compassion and the desire to guide them to Jannah, the eternal paradise.

Even Siddique's bedtime stories were filled with lessons about Da'wah and sharing the message of Islam.

His parents ensured his young heart was filled with love for Allah and a strong desire to bring others closer to Him.

As Siddique grew older and started attending a school with children from various religious backgrounds, he naturally needed to help his friends understand and appreciate Islamic values and customs.

Abdullah and Fatima also taught their children long and heartfelt prayers and enjoyed hearing them reciting them passionately.

Some of the prayers they taught included:

"Ya Allah! Increase my knowledge! Ya Allah! Expand my soul!"

"Ya Allah! You are great! We know nothing except what You have taught us! Surely You are All-Knowing, All-Wise!"

"Ya Allah! Protect my heart from hypocrisy, my actions from malice, and my tongue from lying!"

-

One day, when Siddique came home from school, he shared an experience that filled his parents' hearts with joy.

They praised Allah and made dua for their children, realising that this was the beginning of Siddique's long and noble journey in the path of Da'wah. At that time, Siddique was just past his fifth year.

He recounted his day: "Today, Ahmad, Suresh, and I played together.

I asked Ahmad, 'Do you know Allah?'

He said he did and started telling us about Allah."

Siddique paused for a moment, his eyes shining with excitement. "Then, I got an idea!"

"When Ahmad finished talking about Allah, I told them about Jannah. Even Ahmad didn't know much about Jannah, so I told them all the amazing treasures Allah has kept for us in Jannah."

He continued, "Suresh was listening to what I was saying with great surprise. I think his parents never told him about all this. That's why he listened so carefully when Ahmad and I talked."

Abdullah and Fatima were listening attentively, their faces glowing with pride and happiness.

Siddique added, "Then, the teacher came, and we had to stop talking and listen to her lesson.

"But maybe today, Suresh and Ahmad went home and talked to their parents about what we discussed!"

Hearing this, Abdullah and Fatima realised the beauty of how Siddique, in his innocence, had already started his journey of Da'wah, inviting his friends to learn about Allah and Jannah.

This moment filled their hearts with immense gratitude to Allah, knowing that their son had begun to embrace his role in guiding others to the path of goodness.

-

There was a time when people stopped living peacefully together, and communities began to drift apart.

People started to see people of other territories, communities and religions with hatred, and this negative attitude was typical among everyone.

Feelings of humanity, brotherhood, and the spirit of Da'wah—inviting others to the way of Allah—were becoming weak.

Instead, people began to show more racism, which was evident in their words and deeds.

Unfortunately, this harmful behaviour of the older generation also started affecting the younger generation.

The young were exposed to a harsh way of thinking that showed little kindness, not even toward the elderly.

The culture seemed to be drifting away from the principles of Islamic guidance, and Abdullah was apprehensive about this change.

Abdullah was concerned about ensuring his children grew up with the correct teachings and values.

He and his wife were determined to educate their children properly so that the negative trends around them would not influence them.

They taught their children how to interact with all kinds of people who came to their homes, like beggars, servants, traders, postmen, and people who checked the electricity and water meters.

No matter what religion or background these visitors had, Abdullah and his wife trained their children to treat everyone with the best qualities of humanity and brotherhood.

They taught their children always to show dignity and respect to others. They encouraged them to act kindly and reminded them that such behaviour would bring great rewards in Jannah, eternal paradise.

By instilling these values in their children, Abdullah and his wife hoped to guide them toward becoming compassionate and respectful individuals in society.

-

One hot day, an elderly man was working in the household garden.

He had started early morning, cleaning and tidying up the garden, and worked tirelessly for hours.

Young Siddique watched the old man closely from a window inside the house. He saw the man bending down to pick up leaves, pull weeds, and sweep away dirt.

As time passed, the sun climbed higher in the sky, and the heat grew stronger. The scorching sun made the air thick and heavy.

Even though the heat was unbearable, the elderly man diligently continued his work, occasionally wiping the sweat from his forehead. Siddique saw the man was tired and struggling under the blazing sun.

Siddique felt deeply sad as he watched the old man suffer in the heat. He could not stand the sight of the man's discomfort any longer.

With a sense of urgency, Siddique rushed back to his room and grabbed his small umbrella. He hurried out to the garden where the man was working without hesitating.

Approaching the elderly man respectfully, Siddique held out his little umbrella and kindly said, "Please, Uncle, use this umbrella to protect yourself from the sun while you work."

The old man paused, surprised by this unexpected gesture from a young boy. His eyes softened with joy and gratitude. Siddique's kindness and concern deeply touched him.

With a warm smile, the old man accepted the umbrella and looked at Siddique with admiration.

"Thank you, my son," he said. May you grow up to be a great

person who solves humanity's problems." His words were sincere and a heartfelt blessing.

--

Yes, it seemed that Allah had heard the old man's prayer, and who knows?

Perhaps one day, Siddique will become a beacon of hope and kindness for many people, just as the old man had wished.

SPROUT

Siddique enrolled in the Islamic Children's Circles, run by the village development council and the local National Association for Social Reform unit.

The circle was an excellent opportunity for him and other children to learn and practice the fundamentals of life based on Islamic teachings.

It wasn't just about learning; it provided a healthy environment filled with good friends, guiding them toward producing Good Citizens.

The environment of the circles protected Siddique from the seasonal challenges and pressures that many children face.

It taught him to focus on various aspects of life, from good manners to moral values.

These teachings were theoretical and meant to be lived out in everyday actions and interactions, especially in school.

At the time, Siddique was in the eighth standard in the school. I still remember some of the stories shared by the section head of grade eight, which revealed Siddique's character and how he applied the lessons he learned in the children's circle.

-

One day, the teacher was not present in Siddique's classroom.

With no one to guide them, many students began to talk freely among themselves, some whispering and others chatting loudly.

A few even decided to play games, turning the classroom into a playground.

Suddenly, the section in charge entered the room, and his mere presence brought an immediate hush.

He tapped on the desk loudly.

The sound echoed through the room, and every student froze in their place, stunned.

His deep and commanding voice sent a wave of dread through the room.

Though all the students knew him to be compassionate, his authority was unmistakable at that moment.

"Who is holding a musical concert here?" he shouted, his voice booming. "Who blew the whistle?

Come forward! Otherwise, everyone will have to take a hit!" He slammed the cane on the table as he spoke, adding to the tension in the room.

The students, who had quickly picked up their notebooks and pretended to study, kept their heads down.

None dared to make eye contact or even breathe too loudly. Just then, the section in charge was called away by a teacher in the next classroom.

He left, but the silence he commanded stayed.

Breaking that tense silence, Siddique, who had been sitting quietly all along, suddenly pushed back his chair and stood up.

His eyes were filled with a mix of determination and worry. He quietly left the classroom and headed to the head teacher's desk.

Siddique stood there for a few seconds, silent but visibly shaken. Then, tears began to flow from his eyes.

"Sir! Forgive me..." he said, his voice quivering. "I was the one who blew the whistle. Don't hit others! Hit me!" With tears streaming down his cheeks, he stretched out his hand and stood humbly before the head teacher.

The head teacher, who had never expected such a confession from Siddique, was taken aback.

For a moment, he was speechless. He had always admired Siddique for his attitude, manners, and commitment to his studies, and it was difficult for him to believe that Siddique would do such a thing.

However, Siddique's honesty and courage only deepened the teacher's admiration for him.

He gently touched Siddique's shoulder and asked softly, "Son, why did you whistle in the classroom?"

Still nervous and wiping away his tears, Siddique replied, "I don't know how to whistle. I just tried it. The noise came out without me knowing."

The head teacher smiled warmly, moved by Siddique's virtue of admitting his mistake.

He took Siddique by the hand and walked him back to the classroom. Once there, he gathered all the students' attention.

"Listen, everyone," the head teacher began, his voice steady but kind.

"Today, Siddique has shown us all a great example of honesty and courage. He made a mistake but owned up to it, even when he could have stayed silent. This is the mark of a true character."

He then prayed for Siddique's bright future, asking Allah to guide and bless him.

The children, who already knew Siddique well and respected him, chanted "Amin" in unison, filling the classroom with unity and hope.

--

When Siddique completed his Ordinary Level Examination, it was as if a long-awaited dream had finally come true.

He had been eagerly counting down the days to this moment, looking forward to stepping into the next chapter of his life.

His excitement was evident as he prepared to attend a special training session organised by the Village Development Council.

This wasn't just any ordinary event—it was an opportunity to learn, grow, and connect with the community, and Siddique was determined to make the most of it.

With a big smile and a heart full of enthusiasm, Siddique bid farewell to his Umma and Dad.

They blessed him with warm wishes, knowing how much this training meant to him.

I had the privilege of taking Siddique to the training program. We rode together on my motorcycle. Siddique's excitement was palpable.

His eyes sparkled with anticipation, and he couldn't stop talking about everything he hoped to learn and the people he hoped to meet.

Alhamdulillah, it was a joyful ride, filled with the energy of a young boy ready to embrace the world.

Once we arrived, Siddique threw himself into every activity with great enthusiasm and a thirst for knowledge.

He participated in all the programs as a passive observer and an active learner, eager to absorb every piece of shared wisdom.

His dedication and commitment did not go unnoticed; he quickly became known among the participants for his lively spirit and eagerness to engage.

Those five days were no exaggeration—an actual turning point that cemented Siddique's ambition in life.

They were filled with enlightening talks, practical workshops, and inspiring discussions that opened his eyes to new possibilities and helped him realise his potential.

A special buzz was in the air on the last day of the training session.

Everyone eagerly awaited the final talk by the leader of the Village Development Council.

This leader was known for his wisdom and vision, and his words always touched the hearts of those who listened.

Siddique, of course, was fully prepared. He sat at the front, his notebook and pen ready to capture every word.

-

"Dear youth," the leader's clear and strong voice rang out.

He looked out over the crowd of eager and attentive young faces, their eyes filled with curiosity and anticipation.

"Please listen carefully to what I am about to say and try to keep it in your mind."

He paused, letting his words settle in.

"Think about the current situation of our society," he continued, "not only from what you have learned so far in this program but also from your own experiences, your observations."

"Look around you—on the one hand, there are some outstanding features to be seen! These bring great joy and hope."

The leader's eyes softened as he spoke of the good he saw, but his expression turned serious.

"On the flip side, we see many problems! These problems put us in deep emotional pain and distress."

"The truth is that positive societal changes cannot be brought about unless we carefully consider each issue and make appropriate reform efforts."

"I fear the situation will deteriorate further if we don't think and act like that."

The crowd grew more focused, sensing the importance of his message.

"We must remember," he went on, "that Allah will not change you or the environment in which you live unless you try to change yourself."

"This is the natural law Allah has set for worldly life. If you want to see a better society, a stronger community, a future filled with hope, it starts with each of us taking the first step to change what is within us and around."

He took a deep breath, allowing his words to sink in.

"So, I bring to your attention some basic issues observed in our society and your responsibilities because of them! Listen here!"

The youth leaned in closer, hanging onto his every word.

"Our people's lifestyle is deteriorating," he said, his voice tinged with concern.

"Everyone suffers, especially young men and women, due to external influences. They are losing their way, drifting from the path of righteousness. Therefore, they need to be rescued from this massive moral decline. Our role is to help and guide them to a better way."

He paused, his eyes sweeping over the audience, making sure each one felt the weight of his words.

"Almost everyone's smartphones have become cinemas," he continued.

"Many people spend their time and enjoy watching the ugly things someone does for a living. The actions of our youth bear witness to their hideous effects."

"Many students have lost themselves in this cinema craze, affecting their hearts and minds. They are getting distracted from what truly matters."

"Therefore, they must be re-energized and disciplined through education and good manners."

He let his words resonate for a moment.

"I see people among us," he said, "developing themselves in various fields and living without concern about community development."

"They do not realise their worth and responsibilities; they do not understand the negative impact this neglect will have on the community in the long run."

"Therefore, they must be sensitised, awakened, and encouraged to contribute to social revival work."

The leader's tone became even more passionate as he discussed the deviations in the community due to politics and territories.

"In politics, extreme divisions are deeply entrenched from generation to generation."

"The formation of political parties is to respect people's

differences of opinion when choosing better representatives and ensure better services to the community."

"However, families and friends are torn apart over differences. Political leaders and community must be educated to settle the differences carefully without further dividing our community."

"People show hostility due to the territorial differences."

"This situation weakens the community's strength and seriously damages unity and growth. Leaders and people must be educated to respect the differences."

He sighed deeply.

"Many people are engrossed in selfish lifestyles without any concern for the development and improvement of the nation."

"They are caught up chasing their desires while social evils are unleashed everywhere."

"People must be rescued from that self-destructive state and directed towards a prosperous order of life."

The leader looked around, his gaze resting on each young person as if speaking directly to their hearts.

"We need to build a model of social order that can attract and guide all the people around us who do not know the purpose of life and are drowning in ignorance."

"Every citizen living in this village and country," he emphasised, "is responsible for this.

"As Muslims, this is a life obligation. We cannot sit back and wait for someone else to solve these problems. It is our duty."

He smiled warmly, his eyes filled with hope.

"Dear youth! You are the hope stars of the future! You should think deeply about this."

"Experts, thinkers, and leaders who can lead our society and nation in various fields should emerge from you. You are the ones who will bring about the change we so desperately need."

"You should plan your future based on this mission in mind," he continued.

"Efforts should be made for that. This course you have attended must have given you the basic knowledge and guidance required to shape your personal and community life."

"Use it. Build on it. Grow from it."

His voice softened, carrying a tone of both encouragement and caution.

"This mission before you is not an easy one!"

"It will require effort, patience, and perseverance. But if you prepare, then surely Almighty Allah will be with you!"

"He will stabilise your feet in this work!"

"He will guide, strengthen, and help you succeed."

-

The training workshop concluded with a heartfelt vote of thanks. As the leader's words of gratitude faded, a bustling excitement filled the air.

All the students began to gather their belongings and prepare to head home.

The atmosphere buzzed with chatter and laughter as they shared their experiences from the past few days.

However, amidst this flurry of activity, Siddique alone remained still.

He did not move from his spot. He sat there, his eyes closed, deep in thought.

Time seemed to pass slowly for him, and he appeared to be in his world.

After a while, he finally stood up. Slowly and with a sense of claiming purpose, He began to pray.

His Sajada was long. Then, he plunged into a long, heartfelt Dua.

Those who noticed could see this was not an ordinary prayer but a conversation between a devoted servant and his Creator.

After he finished his Dua, Siddique rose with renewed energy. There was a new light in his eyes—a confidence that seemed to shine from within.

He walked straight to the leader of the village development council.

Without hesitation, he approached, wrapped his arms around him, and gave him a deep, sincere hug.

Surprised at first, the leader smiled warmly, recognising the determination radiating from the young boy.

I saw it, too. The confidence shining on Siddique's face was unmistakable.

His heart had found its purpose. Yes, at the tender age of sixteen, Siddique had set foot on the path of prosperity.

Raised by parents who instilled excellent values and principles in him, Siddique had always carried the vision of Allah's pleasure in his heart.

But this event had struck a chord deep within him. It had powerfully awakened something that had been quietly growing inside him.

Siddique must then have realised that some words he used to hear from his dad in early childhood were more than just words.

They were the seeds of his life's ambition. Those words had now blossomed into a full, clear mission.

Yes! Siddique had declared his life's mission.

The prayer he performed, the long Sajada, the Dua—they were all steps toward making that mission a reality.

However, no one could have heard his declaration at that time. But those close to him, who worked with him closely, would see every subsequent move he made in his life.

Every decision he took bore witness to his mission to be a source of light and guidance for others and to contribute meaningfully to his community and beyond.

--

Until then, Siddique was known only to his family, relatives, classmates, and teachers.

He was a bright, well-mannered boy, but his presence was mostly confined to the circle of people who interacted with him daily.

However, as the years passed, Siddique's influence and reputation spread far and wide across the village.

His character, compassion, and commitment to serving others made him a beloved figure for everyone—children, students, youth, adults, and the elderly.

Even those considered lost causes by society—those abandoned by many as irredeemable—found solace in Siddique's presence.

His humility and kindness had a way of reaching hearts that others could not.

People who had long been written off gained immense respect for Siddique, recognising him as a beacon of hope and guidance.

When the elderly saw Siddique, their faces would light up with happiness.

He was particularly concerned about making them feel heard and valued.

He would listen patiently to their stories, give them his full attention, and express genuine interest in their experiences.

For many, Siddique became a cherished companion who brought joy to their otherwise lonely days. In return, he found a special place in their hearts and duas.

One day, while walking home from the local mosque, Siddique noticed an old man sitting alone under a tree.

This man, named Uncle Kareem, had a reputation for being grumpy and bitter.

Many in the community had given up on him, thinking he was beyond help.

Yet, Siddique saw something different—a soul in need of kindness.

Siddique approached Uncle Kareem without hesitation, greeting him with a warm smile.

"Assalamu Alaikum, Uncle. How are you today?"

Kareem, who had grown accustomed to being ignored, looked up in surprise.

His face softened as Siddique sat beside him, not rushing or showing any signs of impatience.

Someone was giving Uncle Kareem their full attention for the first time in years.

At first, the conversation was slow, with Kareem muttering about his aches and pains.

But Siddique's patience was unwavering. He listened intently as Uncle Kareem spoke of his past—his youth, his work as a carpenter, the family he once had, and the loneliness that had crept in after they moved away.

Siddique didn't interrupt or offer empty platitudes.

Instead, he asked questions, showing genuine interest in the stories Uncle Kareem had kept buried for so long.

The old man's bitter exterior slowly melted away, replaced by a faint smile as he recounted moments of pride and joy from his younger days.

From that day forward, Siddique made it a point to visit Uncle Kareem regularly.

He would bring a small snack, sit under the tree, and listen as Kareem shared more stories from his past.

Soon, the elderly man became a fixture of Siddique's routine, eagerly awaiting his visits.

His once grumpy demeanour was now replaced with anticipation and warmth, knowing someone cared enough to listen.

One evening, as Siddique prepared to leave Uncle Kareem's side after another heartfelt conversation, the old man grabbed his hand gently.

With teary eyes, he whispered, "You have given me more than you know, son. People had forgotten me, but you... you've made me feel alive again. May Allah reward you."

-

Uncle Kareem's words echoed the sentiments of many in the community.

Siddique's humility and kindness had touched hearts in ways few others could.

Those abandoned by society and felt they had no place or value found comfort in his presence.

His character became a beacon of hope, and in return, Siddique earned a special place in their hearts and valuable duas.

--

Those who dreamt of bringing positive societal changes often sought Siddique to share their thoughts.

They found great relief in confiding in him, as though speaking to someone who could truly understand and carry the weight of their hopes and dreams.

Though Siddique was still young, his sincerity and passion gave them hope that their aspirations for a better future might be realised someday.

-

One warm afternoon, a group of village elders gathered under the shade of an ancient oak tree.

The air was filled with the murmur of conversations, but there was a shared sense of anticipation.

They were on their way to visit Siddique, a young man whose wisdom and sincerity had earned him the respect of both the old and young alike.

Those elders had lived long enough to see the many changes in their community, some good, some troubling, but they dreamed of making their society better for future generations.

Siddique welcomed them with warmth and humility.

"Uncles and Aunties, "please come in. How can I be of service to you?"

The eldest, Uncle Ibrahim, stepped forward with a kind smile. "My son, we've come not to ask for anything but to share something close to our hearts."

Siddique led them to a comfortable seating area and offered tea and water.

The elders settled in, each sensing that they were in the presence of someone who would listen.

After a brief pause, Uncle Ibrahim began, "You see, Siddique, we've lived many years and seen much change in our time."

"We've built this village with our hands, raised our children with hopes, yet there's still so much to be done."

"So much that we feel we haven't achieved. Our generation is fading, but our dreams... they remain."

Auntie Fatima, known for her work as a midwife who had delivered many children in the village, added, "We dream of a community where no child goes hungry, where education reaches even the poorest among us, and where respect and kindness are the law of the land. But sometimes, it feels like these dreams will vanish with us."

The other elders nodded in agreement, each one carrying their aspirations.

A retired schoolteacher, Uncle Harun longed for a school in the village where children could receive a quality education.

There was Auntie Mariam, who had spent her life tending to the sick and now hoped for a health clinic where no one would suffer without care.

Siddique listened intently, his face thoughtful but soft with understanding.

He could see how much these aspirations meant to them, how long they had carried these dreams, and how much hope they had placed in a future they might never see.

Yet, they had something else—a sense of trust in him, as though they believed he could carry the torch forward.

"My dear uncles and aunties," Siddique finally said, his voice gentle but firm.

"Your dreams are not small things. They are the seeds of the future. You have spent your lives planting those seeds, and just because you may not see the trees grow does not mean they will not grow."

The elders leaned in, listening closely as Siddique continued. "What you have done for this community—your work, your sacrifices—will not be forgotten."

"I may be young, but others like me will take up the responsibility to continue what you've started."

"Your dreams are now our dreams. InshaAllah, we will build that school, open that clinic, and ensure no child is left behind."

Tears welled up in Auntie Mariam's eyes as she whispered, "You give us hope, Siddique. We've held these dreams for so long, and now it feels like they won't die with us."

Uncle Harun, usually a man of few words, nodded and said, "It's true. We've been looking for someone who could understand the weight of these aspirations, and we've found him in you."

Siddique smiled humbly, feeling the weight of their words and the joy of knowing he could help carry their hopes into the future.

"I am honoured by your trust," he said.

"But know this—these are not just your dreams or mine. They belong to the entire community."

"Together, we will work toward them, and with Allah's help, we will see them come to life."

The elders left Siddique's home that day with lighter hearts. They felt immense relief as though they had passed the torch to someone worthy of carrying it forward.

Siddique watched them leave, his heart whole of both responsibility and inspiration.

-

Siddique used to get these kinds of input, inspiration, and motivation.

He knew the road ahead would be challenging, but he was ready.

The elders' dreams had become his own, and he was determined to work tirelessly to ensure their vision for a better society would one day come to fruition.

--

Siddique became a role model for parents concerned about their children's future.

They saw in him the qualities they wished to cultivate in their children—integrity, dedication, and a sense of purpose.

Many parents encouraged their children to associate with Siddique, believing his positive influence could shape them into better individuals.

-

One evening, as the sun dipped below the horizon, casting a warm golden glow over the village, two worried parents, Mr. and Mrs. Saleh, approached Siddique's home.

Their teenage son, Adil, had recently been falling into bad company and showing signs of rebellion.

Though they had tried everything to guide him back to the right path, their efforts seemed to fall short.

With heavy hearts, they turned to Siddique, the young man whom the entire village admired for his wisdom and integrity.

Siddique welcomed them with his usual calm demeanour, offering tea and a place to sit. After a moment of silence, Mr. Saleh spoke, his voice filled with concern.

"Siddique, we've come to seek your help."

"Our son, Adil... he's lost his way."

"He's fallen in with the wrong crowd, and we fear that he's straying further from the values we've raised him with."

"We know how much the younger generation looks up to you. Could you perhaps spend some time with him? Maybe your influence could help him see the right path."

Mrs Saleh nodded, her eyes filled with worry.

"We've done all we can as parents, but he no longer listens to us. We've heard from many in the village how you've guided other young people. We only hope that he'll listen to you."

Siddique, always humble, listened carefully to their plea. He knew guiding someone required patience and understanding, especially during the turbulent teenage years.

"I understand your concerns," he said gently.

"Teenage years can be challenging for the young person and their parents. But we can help Adil rediscover his purpose with a little effort."

The next day, Siddique approached Adil after school, greeting him with a friendly smile.

Adil was taken aback at first, unsure why Siddique had sought him out.

Despite his reputation as a well-liked and respected figure, Siddique never came across as judgmental or overbearing.

"Assalamu Alaikum, Adil," Siddique said with a calm voice.

"I was wondering if you'd like to go for a walk with me. I could use some company."

Adil, though initially hesitant, agreed. Siddique didn't immediately dive into lectures or criticism as they walked through the village.

Instead, he spoke about martial arts.

Siddique already knew that Adil was interested in martial arts, and

Adil also knew that Siddique was one of the shining martial arts champions in the village.

He emphasised the importance of having a healthy lifestyle to become physically stronger.

He explained how Shaytan's whispers can often lead people astray and how much strength it takes to stay true to one's values.

"What do you want in life, Adil?" Siddique asked as they neared the riverbank.

Adil paused, surprised by the question. "I don't know... I guess I haven't thought about it."

Siddique nodded thoughtfully.

"That's normal at your age. But let me tell you something—it's important to think about it."

"You're at a point in life where your decisions will shape your future."

"The people you surround yourself with and your choices have an impact. I'm not here to lecture you, Adil, but I see potential in you that I don't want to see wasted."

As they continued their conversation, Siddique didn't just discuss what Adil shouldn't do.

Instead, he inspired him to think about his dreams and ambitions.

They spoke of the power of self-discipline and the joy of serving a purpose bigger than oneself.

Over the following weeks, Adil began spending more time with Siddique.

They would discuss everything from faith to ambitions, and Siddique guided Adil without ever making him feel judged or pressured.

Slowly but surely, Adil started to distance himself from the bad influences in his life.

He began focusing on his studies and even took an interest in volunteering at the local Village Development Council, something Siddique had been involved with for years.

Mr. and Mrs. Saleh noticed the change in their son.

One evening, Adil came to his parents and said, "I've been thinking a lot lately. I realise I wasn't being the best version of myself, but I want to change. Siddique helped me see that there's more to life than just following the crowd."

Mrs. Saleh's eyes filled with tears. "And we're so thankful to Siddique for being the guide you needed."

-

Siddique's influence had done more than steer Adil away from the wrong path—it had awakened something deeper within him, a sense of purpose that he would carry for the rest of his life.

For Mr and Mrs Saleh, Siddique had not only helped their son but had given them hope that the younger generation could still grow into the kind of people they had always dreamed of raising: individuals of integrity, dedication, and a sense of purpose.

--

As for the children, Siddique was nothing short of a hero. Whenever they saw him, they would shout his name and cheer excitedly. He always made time for them, even if it was just a few minutes to exchange Salams or ask about their day.

He understood the value of those moments, believing that a small investment of time and kindness could yield great results in the long future.

-

One sunny afternoon, playful laughter filled the air as Siddique strolled through the village.

A group of children playing by the park suddenly spotted him in the distance.

Their faces lit up with joy, and instantly, they began to call out his name.

"Siddique! Siddique bhai!" they shouted; their excitement contagious.

Siddique smiled warmly as he approached them. Even though he had errands to run, he stopped and spent a few moments with the eager children, who now gathered around him like a flock of little birds.

"Assalamu Alaikum, my young friends!" Siddique greeted them cheerfully.

"How's everyone doing today?"

The children's eyes sparkled with happiness. "Wa Alaikum Assalam, Siddique bhai! We're playing a game, but we were waiting for you!" one of the boys said.

Curious, Siddique knelt at their level. "Oh? What game is it?"

"It's hide-and-seek, but we don't have anyone to be 'it'!" a little girl explained.

Siddique chuckled softly.

"Well, it seems like you need someone to take charge. How about I play one round with you all? But only one—I have things to do, you know," he teased.

The children's cheers echoed through the park as they excitedly ran to their hiding spots. Siddique counted aloud, his voice full of playful energy.

As soon as he finished, he began searching for them, knowing where they were but pretending not to notice their obvious hiding places.

His lighthearted approach filled the children with joy.

After the game, Siddique sat with the group and asked about their day, schoolwork, and families.

The children shared stories, giggled at their small victories, and listened intently to anything Siddique said.

One of the boys, Bilal, asked, "Siddique bhai, how come you always make time for us? Aren't you busy?"

Siddique smiled and patted Bilal on the shoulder.

"I may be busy, but spending time with you all is important too. Do you know why?"

"Because every one of you will grow up one day, and these

moments we share now will help shape the kind of person you become."

The children listened carefully, their eyes wide with admiration.

"Remember," Siddique continued, "being kind, taking time to care for others, and being good to one another will make you strong. And one day, you'll do the same for others."

With that, he bid them farewell, promising to play again the next time he had a free moment.

As Siddique walked away, the children waved and shouted his name again, their voices filled with admiration and joy.

-

Siddique knew these little moments of kindness could have a lasting impact, shaping the future of the children he loved so dearly.

And to the children, Siddique wasn't just a friend; he was the hero who made them feel like they mattered.

They found him who always made them feel valued and cared for, even in the smallest moments.

--

Siddique's presence became a constant source of inspiration and hope for everyone in the village.

His journey from a quiet boy known only to a few to a beloved figure embraced by all was a testament to the power of good character, sincerity, and unwavering faith.

Teenagers generally engage in various activities for entertainment, often without much thought beyond immediate enjoyment.

They spend their time on what interests them most, finding satisfaction in these pastimes, sometimes considered notable achievements.

However, Siddique took a different approach to leisure. He consciously aligned his recreational activities with his life mission.

Rather than simply seeking enjoyment, he saw every hobby and skill as a potential tool to serve a greater purpose.

Though Siddique had a particular fondness for reading, he was not limited to that alone.

He was keen on acquainting himself with a broad range of fields, understanding that this diversity of knowledge and skills could help him develop a well-rounded personality capable of working with and leading different kinds of people in the future.

Siddique explored various interests: he painted, composed poems, wrote stories, created songs, and sang.

He learned technical skills, became deeply interested in martial arts, and actively worked on improving his public speaking abilities.

While he did not specialise in every field, he ensured he developed sufficient familiarity with each.

For Siddique, these activities were more than just hobbies—purposeful pursuits and enablers.

He saw them as valuable tools that enabled him to understand better, connect with, and guide others in his future endeavours.

His efforts reflected a deep commitment to self-development and a clear vision of the path he wanted to walk.

--

Siddique was deeply interested in learning the fundamentals of Islam and delved into Islamic history with great enthusiasm.

These studies were not mere academic pursuits for him; they were avenues to better understanding and shaping his destiny.

A significant resource in his journey was the library his father had carefully built over the years.

This collection of books became a cornerstone for Siddique, providing him with a wealth of knowledge.

He maintained a habit of noting the questions and new thoughts that arose during his readings.

These reflections became opportunities for further exploration and personal growth as he sought to share and develop these ideas with others.

However, his approach to learning was not limited to solitary reading; he actively engaged in discussions with knowledgeable individuals, offering in-depth explanations and exchanging ideas.

-

One afternoon, Siddique sat at the Village Development Council library.

He was reading a book, and his notebook was open, jotting down questions and thoughts as he read.

One phrase in a book caught his attention—something about the balance between free will and divine destiny.

Intrigued, Siddique scribbled his questions: "How does one reconcile the two?"

"Can humans truly make choices if Allah predetermines everything?"

He pondered the ideas for a while, but instead of settling on a conclusion right away, he marked the page and made a note to discuss it later.

Later that week, Siddique visited an elderly scholar in the community known for his deep knowledge and wisdom.

After exchanging greetings, Siddique opened his notebook and brought up the question.

"I've been thinking a lot about free will and divine destiny," Siddique began, his eyes filled with curiosity.

"How do we understand both in the context of our faith?"

The scholar smiled, pleased with Siddique's eagerness to explore such complex topics.

"Ah, that's a question many have wrestled with over centuries. Tell me, what have you gathered from your readings so far?"

Siddique explained his thoughts, outlining the different perspectives he had encountered in his books.

He offered his reflections but clarified that he was still seeking a deeper understanding.

The scholar listened carefully, nodding occasionally as Siddique spoke.

After reflection, the scholar responded, "You've raised excellent points, Siddique. The balance between free will and destiny is indeed a profound matter."

"But remember, faith is not just about finding the perfect answers; it's about seeking, questioning, and engaging with the divine mysteries. It's an ongoing journey."

The conversation evolved into a rich discussion, where both Siddique and the scholar shared insights, dissected verses from the Qur'an, and explored historical interpretations.

Each time Siddique asked a new question, the scholar guided him gently, encouraging him to reflect deeper while offering wisdom from his own experiences.

After an hour of discussion, Siddique felt enriched with answers and more questions to pursue.

He thanked the scholar and promised to return once he had explored further.

As he left, notebook in hand, Siddique reflected on how his learning journey had become one of dialogue and exchange.

It wasn't just about collecting knowledge from books—engaging with others, sharpening his understanding, and constantly growing.

His quest for knowledge had become a shared experience where ideas were nurtured, challenged, and expanded, helping him and others in their spiritual and intellectual growth journey.

--

Despite his thirst for knowledge, Siddique was wise in his interactions.

He consciously avoided wasting time in futile debates, recognising that such arguments rarely touched hearts or inspired genuine change.

Instead, he focused on a more profound strategy: winning human hearts and minds.

This approach aligned perfectly with his ambition of guiding others towards positive transformation and spiritual growth.

Teenagers often become easily swayed by emotions, and this vulnerability can affect even those with strong religious inclinations.

It's common to see people within a community harshly criticising societal and traditional issues, asserting that their perspective is the only correct one while dismissing others as wrong.

Such attitudes often lead to numerous divisions and disputes within society.

However, Siddique stood out for his maturity, even during his teenage years.

This composure and wisdom were likely the result of the disciplined upbringing his parents provided. May Allah bless them for their efforts.

Siddique was greatly troubled by the numerous rituals and ceremonies, most of which did not have a strong basis in the religions prevalent in society at the time.

He intensely disliked the ignorance that overshadowed people's thoughts and actions.

Nevertheless, he did not harbour hatred for the innocent individuals caught in these practices. Instead, he chose not to curse or condemn them.

Siddique approached these individuals with sympathy and concern, hoping to guide them towards a better understanding.

He was patient, waiting for the right moment and environment to address the issues.

Moreover, he actively worked to create such opportunities, understanding that meaningful change required timing and a conducive atmosphere.

-

One evening, as Siddique sat in the courtyard of the Mosque, he overheard a heated debate at a nearby.

A group of youth was passionately arguing over a theological issue, their voices rising as each person tried to outshine the others with their knowledge.

"Siddique, come join us!" one of them, Ahmed, called out.

"You're always reading—surely you have something to say about this!"

Siddique smiled politely but shook his head. "Thank you, Ahmed, but I'll pass."

Curious, Ahmed got up and approached Siddique.

"Why not? You know a lot about these things, and your insights would be valuable."

Siddique leaned back in his chair. "It's not that I don't care about the discussion. But these debates rarely change anyone's heart or perspective. Often, they lead to frustration, and everyone leaves feeling unheard."

Ahmed frowned, puzzled by Siddique's response. "But isn't it important to defend what we believe? To prove our point?"

Siddique nodded thoughtfully.

"Yes, but the question is—how do we do that? Engaging in endless arguments rarely opens people's hearts to new ideas."

"Instead of trying to win a debate, I focus on building understanding and trust."

"If you truly want to inspire someone, it's better to win their heart before trying to win their mind."

Ahmed looked back at the group, still embroiled in their discussion. "So, what do you do?"

Siddique smiled gently.

"I listen. I take the time to understand where people are coming from and offer guidance that speaks to them, not just to their logic."

"People are more likely to embrace change when they feel

respected, heard, and understood."

Ahmed was silent for a moment, reflecting on Siddique's words.

"But what if they're wrong? Don't you have a duty to correct them?"

"Of course," Siddique replied.

"But correction without compassion often falls on deaf ears. If I can win their hearts, they'll be more open to hearing what I say. And sometimes, through kindness and patience, people come to the truth independently."

Ahmed nodded slowly, understanding now what made Siddique different.

He wasn't interested in proving himself right or dominating a conversation.

Instead, he focused on genuine connections, planting seeds of thought that would eventually bloom into understanding.

-

Many people in the community admired Siddique's policy on debating theological issues.

He always wanted to follow the guidance of the Qur'an. He understood Almighty Allah commands us to exchange opinions wisely and beautifully.

The objective should not be to humiliate others but to exchange ideas to guide and be guided by others now or in the future.

--

Adolescence is a unique phase of life, filled with various expectations and desires.

Generally, this stage has a constant tug-of-war between knowledge and desires.

More often than not, desire tends to surpass knowledge, as this is how Allah has designed this period of human life.

It is a time of testing, a critical phase where one's faith character is imprisoned.

Because of this, those who manage to drive their youth with integrity and righteousness are promised a high status on the Day of Resurrection.

Like any other young person, Siddique faced the challenges of adolescence and was occasionally swayed by the temptations and tests of this turbulent period.

His desires were strong, pulling him toward paths that, deep down, he knew were wrong.

But then, in those moments of doubt, he would remember the lessons his parents had taught him since childhood.

His father's voice echoed in his mind: "Siddique, Allah is always watching, and the heart that remains true to its principles will always find peace."

However, the intense training and teachings he had received throughout his life enabled him to endure these challenges with remarkable resilience.

It wasn't an easy journey, but his deep commitment to his principles and pure ambition gave him the strength he needed.

His heart, filled with pure intentions and firm principles, was always protected by Allah's love and grace.

As a result, he remained steady and could resist Shaytan's deceptive allure and traps.

By Allah's mercy, Siddique managed to stay on the right path and safely navigate the trials of his youth. Alhamdulillah.

-

One Friday afternoon, after school, his friends gathered at the local café to plan the weekend.

The conversation quickly turned to a secret party happening that night.

"Siddique, you should come. It'll be fun," one of his friends nudged. "Everyone's going, and no one will know if we stay out late."

Siddique's heart skipped a beat. The idea of sneaking out, being part of something thrilling and unknown, sounded tempting.

He had always avoided such gatherings, sticking to what he knew was right, but today, he felt the weight of his curiosity.

For a moment, he considered it. He imagined being at the party, laughing with his friends, and enjoying the thrill of the night.

But deep inside, he felt a quiet discomfort. His mother's voice echoed in his mind: "Siddique, be mindful of your choices. You know that the hereafter holds far more than this world ever can."

His friends were still talking, the excitement in their voices drawing him in.

But Siddique knew he was standing at a crossroads.

He felt a tug-of-war between the desire to belong and the knowledge that this was a test.

A verse from the Qur'an came to his mind: "And those who guard their chastity... they will be among the righteous."

Quietly, Siddique stood up. "I can't come," he said, forcing a smile. "I promised my parents I'd help them tonight."

His friends gave him a hard time, trying to convince him otherwise.

But Siddique's mind was made up. He excused himself and left the café, the sound of their laughter lingering behind him.

Walking home, he felt both relief and a strange heaviness. The pull of temptation had been strong, and he knew it wouldn't be the last time he faced it.

--

Generally, students view university admission as a significant milestone in their lives.

Many aim to become doctors, engineers, lawyers, or accountants and are encouraged to pursue these prestigious professions from a young age.

When Siddique received the announcement of his excellent results in the A/L examinations, his joy was not driven by worldly desires. Instead, he saw it as a crucial step in his journey.

Many people fondly remember university life for the sense of freedom it brings. For some, the ability to live without the constant oversight of parents or the constraints of village norms adds to the allure.

They revel in the freedom to dress, behave, and live according to their preferences, unburdened by external scrutiny.

Unfortunately, this newfound freedom can also make them vulnerable to the temptations of Shaytaan.

However, Siddique's experience at university was quite different. Unlike many, he was aware of Allah's constant presence and supervision.

He understood that Allah was observing his every action and that he would have to account for his life before Him.

This divine consciousness guided him throughout his university years, ensuring his actions were filled with holiness and maturity.

Siddique pursued his higher education through a government-sponsored free education scheme, which covered his tuition but left him responsible for other expenses.

Understanding his parents' financial obligations toward his siblings, Siddique decided to cover his costs to ease their burden.

He was highly disciplined in managing his finances.

Siddique maintained a detailed record of all his expenses in a notebook, reviewing it monthly, and practised exceptional frugality.

Despite having a modest income, he consistently met his financial needs.

-

One afternoon during his first semester at university, Siddique noticed a flyer on the student board after attending a lecture.

The local library sought part-time help organising books, assisting with cataloguing, and helping visitors.

It wasn't much, just a few hours each week, but it seemed the perfect opportunity.

Siddique applied immediately and, after a brief interview, was hired. The pay wasn't high, but it was enough to cover his basic needs.

With his new job, Siddique quickly developed a routine.

Every morning, he attended classes and studied, and in the evenings, he headed to the library for his shift. Although it was tiring to balance work and academics, Siddique remained determined.

He brought his quiet discipline to the library, ensuring every task was done thoroughly, often impressing his supervisors with his diligence.

But this was only the beginning. Siddique also started tutoring A/L students online.

Word spread that Siddique was knowledgeable and patient, and soon, he had a small group of students paying him for weekly tutoring sessions. The extra income was a blessing.

--

In addition to his financial prudence, Siddique made fasting a regular practice.

He used it to control his desires and maintain discipline in an environment where temptations were prevalent.

For Siddique, fasting was not just a religious ritual but a strategic tool, guided by the Prophet (PBUH), to remain steadfast and resilient against the challenges posed by his surroundings.

--

At just twenty years old and in his second year of university, Siddique received the devastating news that his father had suffered a heart attack and was hospitalised.

The situation was stable, but Siddique was deeply shaken. He felt no one could truly understand his turmoil except Allah, the All-Knowing.

With unwavering faith, Siddique turned to Allah for solace. He prepared himself for Salah, his eyes filled with tears as he poured out his heart in a long and earnest Sajada. His prayers were heartfelt and profound:

"Ya Allah! I do not fear if my dad's life is to end, for You control the span of each life. But my concern is for his afterlife. Ya Allah! Forgive him for both his known and unknown mistakes. Acknowledge all the good he has done. Make him a worthy servant of Yours."

Siddique's faith was such that he began mentally preparing himself for the worst, although there were no definitive signs from the doctors.

He had a deep-seated feeling that his father might not survive much longer.

The following day, Siddique received the news that his father had passed away.

He took on the immense responsibility with great composure. Siddique bathed his father's body, led the funeral prayer, and personally buried him.

He wept and prayed fervently for his father's peaceful afterlife.

Despite his profound grief, Siddique remained committed and mature. Seeing his family enveloped in sorrow, he took it upon himself to guide them through their grief:

"Who can change Allah's will? All we can do now is strive to enhance the afterlife of our Father with the sweet pleasures of Allah's mercy."

"This is our most significant debt of gratitude to him. Let us fully commit to transforming our lives and society to meet Allah's expectations."

Only by doing so can we ensure a peaceful afterlife for our father. This is how we fulfil our debt of gratitude."

Siddique's father's legacy was spoken of with great reverence in the following days.

The phrase, "Siddique's dad is a very blessed person," became popular, leading many parents to reflect on their children's concerns and aspirations.

--

Siddique's university life was marked by a deep commitment to his studies and a genuine desire to make a positive impact.

He never missed a lecture, fully immersed himself in the learning process, and diligently sought clarification from lecturers whenever he encountered doubts.

His focus and dedication set him apart from many of his peers.

While other students might have engaged in the usual university distractions, Siddique remained steadfast in his mission.

He was respected and admired for his exceptional qualities and willingness to help others.

His peers recognised his dedication and often sought assistance in understanding complex subjects.

Siddique's efforts were not just limited to his academic growth; he was deeply invested in his fellow students' intellectual and moral development, who would eventually become key figures in shaping the nation's future.

As Siddique approached his second year at university, he was well-known among his peers for his academic achievements and unwavering principles.

The beginning of each academic year brought a tradition that many students dreaded—the ragging period.

Filled with anticipation and anxiety, new students faced the ritualistic pranks and initiation challenges that upperclassmen often imposed.

But Siddique had a different vision.

He saw this time not as an opportunity to perpetuate the cycle of intimidation but as a chance to make a meaningful impact.

Understanding how overwhelming the transition to university life could be, he resolved to use his position to guide and support the newcomers instead.

Through this practice, Siddique helped many students envision their future meaningfully and plan to use university life effectively.

-

One evening, Siddique observed some new students walking nervously down the hostel corridor, heading towards the senior students' rooms.

It was common for seniors to initiate a hazing ritual with freshers each evening, and Siddique noticed the newcomers' faces displaying palpable fear.

Approaching them, Siddique asked where they were headed.

The students explained that they were going to meet specific seniors. With a reassuring smile,

Siddique invited them to accompany him to his room instead.

Though hesitant and intimidated by the customs, the students could not help but refuse Siddique's request and follow him.

Upon entering Siddique's room, the students promptly sat down on the floor, a customary sign of respect to seniors during that time.

Siddique, well aware of their anxiety and discomfort, decided to shift the focus of the encounter.

He began by asking about their backgrounds, interests, and talents, seeking to understand each student's unique qualities.

After gathering this information, Siddique assigned them a coursework assignment to be submitted within a week, adhering to standard academic formats.

The unexpected assignment took aback the students, as they had not encountered anything like it in the past few weeks.

However, they soon found themselves intrigued and excited by the task, as it presented an opportunity to explore their interests and develop their skills.

Siddique asked them about their experiences and insights gained through the exercise when they completed and submitted their agreed-upon assignments.

The students realised that Siddique's intention was not to demean them through hazing but to guide them towards reflecting on their future and mastering the art of academic writing.

--

Siddique's influence extended beyond his time at university.

His commitment to promoting a sense of purpose and responsibility in others bore fruit in the form of numerous professionals and community leaders who now contribute to society's well-being.

These individuals, many of whom occupy prominent positions, are a testament to Siddique's tireless efforts and profound impact on those around him.

Siddique's journey continued as he pursued higher education at an international university.

During this time, he excelled academically and thrived in extracurricular activities.

He participated actively in various events, particularly those to foster networks among international students and global organisations.

These experiences allowed Siddique to step onto the international stage, where he began to shape his personality and leadership skills.

It was an exciting period of growth for him—one that broadened his horizons and deepened his understanding of different cultures and perspectives.

-

Siddique was thriving in his international university, juggling demanding coursework with a growing enthusiasm for extracurricular activities.

The campus was always bustling with events, and Siddique wanted to seize every opportunity to make his mark.

One day, the university announced an exciting event: a "Global Problem-Solving Challenge," where students from different countries would present solutions to real-world issues.

Teams were encouraged to think creatively and propose anything from simple ideas to grand strategies.

Siddique signed up without hesitation and never shied away from a challenge.

His team decided to tackle an issue close to their hearts: improving access to clean drinking water in remote areas.

They spent weeks brainstorming, gathering research, and preparing their presentation.

They devised a simple but impactful solution: a portable, affordable water filter that could be easily distributed in rural communities.

The big day arrived, and the hall was buzzing with excitement. Teams from all over the world were presenting innovative solutions, and Siddique's turn was fast approaching.

When it was time, Siddique finally stepped onto the stage with his team. Everything was going smoothly—until it wasn't.

Midway through the presentation, the demonstration of their water filter suddenly stopped working.

The water wasn't filtering through as expected and seemed like a complete failure. The audience sat silently, watching how the team would react.

But instead of panicking, Siddique took a deep breath and turned to the audience with a big smile.

"Well, looks like even our filter is a bit thirsty today!" he joked, drawing laughter from the crowd.

He used the unexpected malfunction to explain the importance of persistence in problem-solving.

"Sometimes, even the best ideas have hiccups," he said, "but that's how we learn to improve things."

The audience was impressed by the idea and Siddique's ability to stay calm under pressure.

He turned what could have been an embarrassing failure into a teachable moment, emphasizing that the improvement process often involves setbacks.

In the days that followed, Siddique's presentation became the campus talk.

He was invited to join various student committees, collaborate on projects, and attend international forums.

His ability to adapt and think on his feet earned him admiration from students and professors alike.

That unexpected glitch in the presentation launched Siddique into a broader network of international students and organisations.

He built relationships with people from different fields, expanding his connections and learning from diverse perspectives.

Siddique's story inspired many.

It showed that staying positive and thinking creatively can turn setbacks into opportunities even when things don't go as planned.

For students hoping to make their mark, Siddique's experience reminded them that confidence, adaptability, and a sense of humour can take you far—sometimes farther than a flawless presentation ever could.

-

This chapter of his life played a crucial role in preparing him for the challenges that lay ahead.

He built valuable connections and learned to navigate the complexities of the global arena.

"Uncle!" I exclaimed, taken aback by his words. "It is amazing to hear your story. I wonder if such youth still exist today."

I said, "I understand. His parents and the guidance he received from the village development council significantly shaped Siddique's transformation into a visionary leader."

Inspired by his narrative, I eagerly asked, "Could you tell me more about some of his work?"

Uncle placed his hands firmly on the root of the tree he was leaning against, his gaze tracing it from top to bottom as if drawing wisdom from it. After contemplating, he turned to me with a gleam in his eyes.

"Brother," he began with a sense of anticipation, "the story of Siddique's work is indeed a delicious tale to tell and listen to—a history that is essential for anyone involved in social reform to know."

He leaned in slightly as if preparing to share something profound. "Listen closely to what I'm about to tell you!"

TREE

In those days, hidden forces, supported by external powers and some politicians, were at work, striving to break apart the harmony people had lived with for centuries.

Those efforts sought to fuel rifts among communities that had coexisted peacefully, attempting to ignite division where unity had long prevailed.

It was a time of tension and unease, where every action seemed to carry the weight of potential conflict.

Amidst this backdrop, a grand conference was organised under the theme "A Flourishing Nation."

The event was arranged with great fanfare, drawing in crowds from around the country.

The atmosphere buzzed with anticipation as attendees waited for the special speaker to take the stage.

This speaker was a renowned professor who was recently famous for his bold ideas about modernism and the future.

His words resonated deeply with many, especially the youth, who found his vision for a new way of life captivating.

His rise to prominence had been swift, and his following had snowballed.

He began his speech, moving swiftly and smoothly from one point to another.

His delivery was compelling and brisk, with logical arguments that kept the audience hooked.

His expertise in psychology shone through; he knew how to captivate his listeners, tugging at their emotions and thoughts.

The crowd was spellbound as he spoke, hanging on his every word.

The professor began by addressing the future of the country. His tone was positive and forward-looking, and he spoke of growth, progress, and the potential for greatness.

His words seemed to promise a bright future for everyone. But as his speech progressed, it took a subtle turn.

Slowly but surely, he began to weave in criticisms of the people's traditional and cultural practices.

While still coated in the language of progress and modernism, his words started to target traditional and religious norms and values, particularly those of Islam.

By the end of his speech, it became clear that his message was not just about a prosperous nation but about abandoning longstanding traditions, beliefs, and practices.

He incited racial and religious sentiments, suggesting that these were obstacles to national unity.

His criticism became so pointed that one might wonder if the speech's theme attacked religious values rather than the nation's flourishing.

His harsh and unfounded criticisms of Islam stirred both enthusiasm and anger among the crowd. To his admirers, it was as if he had spoken with undeniable truth and courage.

He concluded with a powerful declaration: "If our country wants real peace and development, its people must be united. If traditional, cultural, or religious differences hinder this, we should leave them aside."

"We must come together towards a modern way of thinking and lifestyle, one preferred by the next generation and practised by the developed world."

"Only through such a change can we establish permanent peace in our country! It can take the country on the path of progress!"

His voice grew heavier as he drove home his point, leaving the crowd excitedly buzzing.

The hall erupted with noise and applause from his followers, their cheers shaking the conference room walls.

Amid this uproar, the program coordinator—an ardent supporter of the professor—rose to his feet.

He lavishly praised the professor.

Then, he announced, "Those who wish to comment on the speech now delivered are invited. We cordially invite anyone who can respond to the Professor's discussions. We always welcome alternative ideas!"

The atmosphere shifted as the attention turned to the leaders representing various religious groups present in the hall.

They had been listening intently, their faces growing paler with every passing minute as the speech delved deeper into atheistic themes and attacked the core values that upheld individual dignity, family harmony, and community unity.

It was clear that none of them had anticipated such a blatant assault on their beliefs at this conference.

The tension was palpable. For the Muslims gathered there, especially the community leaders on the dais, the situation felt like a trap.

They seemed paralysed, sitting in stunned silence, unable to muster the strength to stand up and speak.

The weight of the professor's words had left them numb and confused.

No one dared to say a word, and their silence seemed to drag on, every minute feeling like an eternity.

Sensing the awkwardness, the program coordinator stood up again and announced, "According to our agenda, we had allotted several minutes for comments.

However," he continued with a sly smile, "it seems no one wishes to speak. Perhaps everyone agrees with the professor's views?"

His gaze swept over the dignitaries on the platform, clearly signalling that it was time to move on. His words carried an unspoken challenge—almost a taunt—daring anyone to disagree.

At that moment, a figure quietly rose from the front row. It was Siddique, a young man who had remained silent and composed until then.

His presence had gone largely unnoticed, but now all eyes were on him. As he walked toward the podium, the crowd's murmurings fell silent.

Who was this young man who dared to speak up in such a charged atmosphere?

Although relatively unknown among socio-political leaders, Siddique had a rare clarity of purpose and conviction.

By the grace of Allah, he stepped forward to claim the honour of voicing the truth for the sake of real peace in the nation.

His calm and confident demeanour drew the attention of every soul in the hall. As he stood at the podium, the faces of those who had lost hope and felt trapped began to light up with a renewed sense of optimism.

--

Siddique stood tall at the podium, his face serene. With a calm yet powerful voice, he began praying.

"May the peace and tranquillity of almighty God be upon all those present at this conference."

His words carried a warmth that immediately softened the charged atmosphere. His demeanour was without hesitation or nervousness. Instead, his face radiated confidence, and his voice was steady and clear.

Everyone in the hall was on the edge of their seats, waiting to hear what Siddique would say.

How would he respond to the professor's seemingly logical and persuasive arguments?

What could he say to counteract the condition the professor had stirred up? The anticipation was palpable.

Siddique began his remarks with a calm yet profound statement: "The development of our country is the development of the people living there. Establishing peace and tranquillity in our country means establishing peace and tranquillity in the souls of the people living here."

His voice was smooth and fluent, his words simple yet powerful.

He spoke of things familiar to everyone—things they had perhaps taken for granted—but there was something different in how he articulated them.

It was as if he were breathing new life into old truths.

People listened intently, hanging on every word. Siddique wasn't directly countering the professor's arguments; instead, he was dismantling the foundation on which those arguments were built.

The professor's views were based on a series of misconceptions, presented as simple questions that had taken root in people's minds and hearts over time.

Siddique wasn't merely debating but guiding the audience toward clarity, exposing the ignorance beneath the surface.

Many in the crowd wondered, "How does this man know the deep-seated issues that trouble our hearts?"

They could see that Siddique was addressing problems they had struggled with for years, which seemed almost impossible to solve.

His words felt like a balm to their weary souls, as though he offered answers to questions they had grappled with for ages.

The crowd listened intently, caught up in the rhythm of his speech as if they had lost themselves in his words.

Siddique's voice grew stronger as he declared, "The only way to establish permanent peace and social harmony in our souls and our country is to return to our Creator!"

He spoke with such conviction that it felt like a wave of clarity washed over the room.

With simple examples and logical reasoning, he made them understand God's purpose for humanity and the dangers of straying from it.

With a robust and emphatic conclusion, he said, "If the soul of every person in this country is to find peace, those souls must seek their Creator!

The Creator must restore us! We must understand God's way of life and build our lives based on it."

The conviction in his words seemed to touch every heart present in the congregation. There was a stillness in the room—a quiet realisation.

Everyone there began to reflect deeply on their own lives and the direction they were heading. It seemed as if time had stopped momentarily, and every person in that vast hall was contemplating.

Then, as if moved by a collective spirit, the crowd erupted.

The hands of the thousands gathered instinctively came together in applause, and a wave of joy and cheer spread throughout the hall.

Their faces lit up with newfound hope and realisation. It was as if they had discovered a priceless treasure they had been searching for all their lives.

Siddique's words countered the professor's speech and awakened something deep within the people—a longing for true peace, harmony, and a meaningful life anchored in divine guidance.

--

"May Almighty Allah reward Siddique's parents abundantly!" the people would say, reflecting on this remarkable young man's incredible character and unwavering principles.

It was evident to all those that his parents' prayers, desires, and relentless efforts played a crucial role in shaping Siddique into the amazing personality and exemplary citizen he had become.

They had instilled in him a sense of purpose and a deep commitment to the community and the nation.

Siddique had embraced the weight of the community's and the nation's struggles with a determination and passion that few could match.

The event where he boldly stood up and voiced his truth was the beginning of his journey.

It announced his intent to dedicate his life to guiding others toward true peace and understanding.

Siddique was raised with a clear ambition from a young age. The careful nurturing, coaching, and guidance he received from his parents and mentors shaped his worldview.

He was trained in various fields—intellectually, morally, and spiritually—which gave him the courage and resilience to face such daunting challenges.

Days turned into weeks and months, but Siddique remained steadfast in his mission.

He tirelessly gave intellectual responses to arguments that questioned traditional norms, cultural values, and, specifically, Islamic teachings and the way of life of Muslims.

His words were not merely reactive; they were proactive and transformative.

He didn't just respond to criticisms; he posed deeper questions, encouraging people to reflect on their lives and futures. His approach was not aggressive but rather enlightening.

His ability to touch the core of human consciousness was so impactful that even people of other religions were drawn to his works.

Right-minded writers and scholars often quoted Siddique's thoughts in their writings.

They would dedicate entire pages to discussing his contributions, analysing his ideas, and promoting his vision of unity and harmony.

His writings spread far and wide, carried by the admiration of those who valued his deep insights.

Even magazine publishers, who typically focused on more commercial content, were compelled to publish Siddique's works.

Recognising their profound influence, his views and opinions on the prevailing issues in society became a topic of curiosity, even among those who initially may have disagreed with him.

Media channels soon noticed Siddique's growing popularity and invited him to participate in talk shows and discussions.

Some channels viewed this as an opportunity to boost their ratings, while others sought to challenge and discredit his ideas.

However, Siddique never shied away from these platforms. He saw them as opportunities to spread his message of peace and understanding.

Whenever honest-thinking journalists or media professionals sought his advice or guidance, Siddique organised special sessions and spoke openly and sincerely about the issues that mattered most.

Social media platforms became another powerful avenue for Siddique's message. Influencers began posting clips of his speeches and interviews, which quickly garnered hundreds of thousands of views.

These clips spread like wildfire, reaching deep into the hearts and minds of people, especially the youth.

Through these videos, many began to see Siddique as a beacon of hope, someone who could articulate the values and principles they longed for but couldn't find in the chaos of modern life.

The more his message spread, the more people joined in, embracing his call for purity of thought and true peace.

The youth who benefited from Siddique while he was at university and those associated with him in community work became his partners and team.

His influence grew beyond mere admiration; it became a movement.

People from all walks of life—students, professionals, community leaders, and even those who had initially opposed him—found common ground in his words.

His vision resonated with a universal desire for understanding, compassion, and unity.

Through these efforts, the rising tide of misguidance and divisive slogans began to subside. In this way, Siddique defended his faith and cultural values and became a unifying force.

The country's people's way of life had long been rooted in their traditional culture.

This culture was their foundation, guiding their daily lives, relationships, and values—however, not all aspects of this way of life aligned with human intellectual norms.

There were specific practices and beliefs that, upon closer inspection, seemed irrational or outdated.

Yet, even among the educated, there was a diligent adherence to these traditions, often followed with great care and without questioning their relevance or practicality.

The problematic or retrogressive nature of these customs was mainly ignored; instead, people accepted them as an inevitable part of life, ingrained deeply in their societal fabric.

However, everything changed when the waves of "modernism" began to wash over the country.

People were suddenly forced to confront the issues hidden within their traditions and culture for so long.

These challenges, presented in the name of modern thinking and progress, compelled them to re-evaluate the customs they had once considered sacred.

While some aspects, particularly those relating to the family unit—like marriage and relationships—seemed harmless or even beneficial on the surface, the impact of these traditions began to show cracks when viewed through a modern lens.

The harmonious social order that once prevailed started to unravel.

With these shifts came real consequences. The number of divorces rose sharply as the traditional views on marriage were questioned and challenged.

Family disputes over land and marriage became common, consuming much of people's thoughts and energy.

What were once peaceful communities turned into battlegrounds, where terrible clashes erupted between families.

Crimes such as murders, robberies, and suicides became daily news, a grim reflection of the growing chaos within society.

This turbulence affected the younger generation, particularly students. Frustrated students' academic attitudes began to deteriorate as they became increasingly disconnected from their roots and overwhelmed by the societal changes around them.

The cracks in the parent-child relationship widened as both generations struggled to reconcile their conflicting views on tradition and modernity.

Many of the youth, swept up in the allure of what was presented as "modern fashion," adopted ugly and detrimental habits, thinking them to be signs of progress and freedom.

Moral decay became rampant in educational institutions, where love affairs and reckless behaviour were now commonplace.

In response to this rapidly changing landscape, a television service launched a program to discuss the country's current state and future.

It was an opinion exchange platform, inviting viewers to engage in debates and dialogues about the nation's direction.

This program quickly became popular, resonating with a broad audience who loved hearing different perspectives and ideas.

Siddique, a respected community leader, was invited to participate in this program.

The event brought together various professionals and religious figures, each offering suggestions and proposals for navigating the country's challenges.

Siddique's participation in these discussions proved pivotal.

Siddique didn't just provide surface-level solutions or echo common sentiments; he presented deep, thoughtful insights addressing the root causes of society's issues.

-

The family is the cornerstone of any society and the foundation for a healthy community.

When the family unit thrives, society prospers; when it falters, society also begins to crumble.

Therefore, a nation's well-being is intrinsically linked to the strength and stability of its families.

Ensuring the family unit is nurtured with love, respect, and shared responsibility is crucial.

In every family, the husband or father should take on the primary leadership role, guiding the family with wisdom and care.

However, this leadership is not about control but creating a harmonious environment where all members, including the wife or mother, play an active and supportive role.

For a family to thrive, there must be a foundation of love and warmth where each member feels valued and understood.

Open communication, mutual discussion, and a willingness to compromise are essential.

These qualities help to build a strong bond among family members, fostering an atmosphere where problems are discussed openly and solutions are reached collectively.

By embracing these values, families can restore their internal harmony and, in turn, contribute positively to the broader social fabric.

These principles must be included in school curricula to ensure they are upheld and passed on to future generations.

Educating young minds about the importance of a strong family structure grounded in love, respect, and shared responsibility will help cultivate a new generation that values and protects the family unit.

Schools should actively teach these values, incorporating them into lessons emphasising the importance of empathy, cooperation, and understanding within a family.

Additionally, it is vital to support newly married couples as they embark on their journey of building a family.

Nationwide workshops focusing on these themes should be organised, providing couples with the tools and knowledge to build a solid and loving partnership.

These workshops can offer guidance on effective communication, conflict resolution, and the importance of shared goals and responsibilities, helping couples establish a solid foundation for their future together.

Furthermore, all forms of media should be harnessed to promote and reinforce these noble ideals. From television shows to social media platforms, there should be a concerted effort to sensitise people to the importance of a healthy family unit.

Literature, art, and entertainment should convey positive messages about family values, shaping public perception and encouraging a culture that cherishes and upholds these principles.

On the other hand, any form of art or literature that seeks to devalue or undermine these ideals must be carefully regulated and, if necessary, prohibited.

By taking these steps, society can ensure that the family, as the basic unit of social life, remains strong, healthy, and vibrant, paving the way for a more harmonious and prosperous future for all.

-

Childbearing and childrearing are sacred responsibilities, yet their sanctity seems to have faded in our society today.

Bringing a new human being into the world for the betterment of humanity is perhaps the highest contribution anyone can make. This is a principle that every parent must deeply consider.

Parenthood is more than just an act of creation; it is a lifelong commitment to nurturing, guiding, and shaping the next generation into righteous and virtuous citizens who contribute positively to society.

The existence of elderly homes starkly reminds us of the consequences of neglecting these responsibilities.

While such institutions provide a necessary service for some, they also serve as a glaring lesson for young parents.

The need for elderly homes is a source of shame for our nation; it is a sign of the erosion of the family unit's integrity.

These homes indicate the breakdown in the parent-child relationship, reflecting a broader societal decline.

When parents fail to grasp the true essence of their role, focusing merely on the basics of child-rearing—such as feeding, clothing, and schooling—the result is what we see today: a generation that is often detached from its elders.

It is worth asking why the children you raised with such care and attention now seem to disregard you.

Why do they see you as a burden?

Why are they eager to live apart from you, often choosing to distance themselves as much as possible?

Many parents do not consider these questions until it is too late.

The answer lies in the core of how children are raised. While parents may have nurtured their children physically, providing them with food, clothing, and education, many have overlooked the importance of instilling in them the true purpose of life.

Often, parents are too occupied with their daily lives or unaware of the more profound responsibilities of raising a child.

They fail to teach their children about the spiritual and moral teachings that give life meaning and direction.

Without a foundation rooted in the teachings of the Creator, who has created life and death, children grow up without a sense of purpose or understanding of their true responsibilities.

To remedy this, young parents must revisit the sanctity of their roles.

They must understand that raising a child goes beyond providing material needs; it involves cultivating a deep spiritual and moral consciousness.

Only then can we hope to restore the true purpose of life and rebuild the strong, loving family bonds that are the foundation of a prosperous society.

-

Why do the children, born from the same womb and raised together, end up fighting over their parents' property?

Why do they turn to the police and the courts to resolve a matter of familial harmony and mutual respect?

These questions point to a deep-rooted problem in how our society handles such issues.

Indeed, the rules and customs we have established for distributing inheritance have often only added to the discord and confusion among families.

Rather than being a source of unity, the question of inheritance has become a catalyst for division, jealousy, and strife.

Siblings who once grew up together in love and companionship now become adversaries, driven by a sense of entitlement or perceived injustice.

This sad reality underscores a much larger issue: our community cannot thrive without aligning itself with the divine teachings of the Almighty Creator.

Only He knows us intimately—our desires, fears, flaws, and potential for greatness. His guidance clarifies how to manage our affairs, including the fair and just distribution of wealth after one's passing.

The Creator's teachings are not just about worship; they encompass every aspect of human life, including social and economic matters.

His divine guidance solves our most challenging issues, promoting fairness, compassion, and justice. We inevitably fall into chaos and conflict when we deviate from these teachings.

No matter how well-intentioned, the rules we make in ignorance often lead to unintended consequences that further divide us.

When we align our lives with His guidance, we find solutions to our problems and the strength to build a society grounded in true unity and purpose.

--

Siddique's approach to societal issues was holistic rather than piecemeal.

His commitment to perfectionism was evident in his comprehensive and pragmatic approach to change, addressing the roots rather than just the symptoms of societal problems.

His ideas were deeply rooted in universal values directly aligned with Islamic principles, which advocate for justice, compassion, and integrity in every aspect of life.

This alignment with core Islamic principles captured the attention and admiration of many.

Newspapers played a significant role in popularising Siddique's views and spreading his message to a broader audience.

In those days, Siddique's name was frequently spoken on the tongues of many people throughout the country—a testament to the profound impact of his words and actions.

Alhamdulillah, his influence reached far and wide.

As Siddique continued to gain a following of thousands, his influence expanded beyond the intellectual and spiritual realms.

His leadership, vision, and commitment to positive change did not spare even the country's political landscape.

His presence and thoughts permeated all layers of society, including its leadership.

A television debate on the 'Women Dress Code' held between Siddique and a modernist team was a remarkable example of Siddique's achievements.

-

***Host**: Welcome to tonight's debate on women's dress code and its societal impact.*

On one side, we have Siddique, a respected advocate for traditional dress codes.

Conversely, we have the Modernist team, who argue for a more contemporary approach.

Let's start with the opening statements.

***Modernist**: Thank you.*

We believe that we need to adopt modern lifestyles for society to progress.

For example, in women's dress codes, sticking to traditional styles can limit women's opportunities in various professions.

Modern dress codes, less restrictive, allow women to engage more fully in different careers and roles, leading to innovation and progress.

***Siddique**: Thank you.*

While I understand the Modernist team's view, I want to highlight the importance of traditional dress codes, especially within Islamic guidelines.

These guidelines are not just about clothing but also reflect deeper values of modesty and respect.

They ensure that individuals maintain dignity and ethical principles essential for personal and societal well-being.

***Modernist**: Siddique, isn't it true that traditional dress codes can limit women's opportunities?*

In today's fast-paced world, shouldn't women be able to wear what is practical for their jobs?

Doesn't focusing on dress distract from their skills and capabilities?

***Siddique**: Traditional dress codes, especially in Islam, are designed to respect personal dignity while allowing for professional success.*

For instance, the basic rules of Islamic dress for women include covering the body modestly and not drawing attention. It's not about wearing a black abaya; it's about covering the body respectfully and appropriately.

Women can wear various styles that meet these guidelines and still excel in their careers.

Modesty and professionalism can go hand in hand.

***Modernist**: But isn't sticking to traditional dress codes a way to alienate women from new opportunities?*

The global workplace often has different expectations, and adapting to these can be crucial for career advancement.

***Siddique**: The goal is to balance personal values with professional growth.*

Traditional dress codes are not meant to restrict but to create an environment where values are respected.

Women following these codes have succeeded in many fields, proving that modesty and professional achievement coexist.

The real challenge is finding ways to integrate traditional values with modern needs.

***Modernist**: Don't modernising dress codes reflect society's evolving nature and the need for inclusivity?*

Siddique: Inclusivity doesn't mean abandoning values but integrating them to fit contemporary contexts.

Traditional dress codes can be adapted while still respecting cultural values.

The aim is to find a balance where values and modern advancements support each other.

Doing so can create a society that respects individuality while promoting respect and dignity.

***Host**: Thank you, Siddique and the Modernist team, for this thoughtful discussion.*

Let's hear your closing statements.

***Modernist**: We recognise the importance of values and respect in society.*

While we initially focused on modernising dress codes, we now see the importance of integrating ethical principles with modern practices.

Siddique's points have helped us understand how tradition and modernity can work together.

***Siddique**: I appreciate the Modernist team's openness.*

This debate shows we can maintain our values while adapting to modern advancements.

Thank you for the opportunity to discuss this critical topic, and I hope it encourages more thoughtful consideration of how tradition and progress can benefit everyone.

***Host**: Our debate has concluded.*

Thank you both for your contributions. We hope this discussion has provided insight into balancing tradition and modernity in women's dress codes. Good night.

The media fervently broadcast that the country's economic growth indicators had reached unprecedented levels.

However, the reality on the ground told a different story.

The cost of living was crushing the people like never before. Many struggled to make ends meet, with incomes falling short of covering necessities.

This economic strain had a cascading effect, leading to various social issues.

Bribery, which had become an unofficial "special allowance" for most government employees, was so widespread that both the givers and takers seemed to have lost any sense of guilt.

Corruption was no longer an exception; it was perceived as a norm.

Meanwhile, the frequency of theft and looting was rising. News of houses and shops being broken into became a daily occurrence and often made it to the front pages of magazines.

Poor families, unable to provide their children with nutritious food, found themselves in dire straits.

To make matters worse, the skyrocketing prices of essential medicines added another layer of hardship.

Meanwhile, the affluent and the philanderers showed no interest in society's plight.

Ill-minded politicians were engrossed in their worldly pursuits, seemingly oblivious to the problems unfolding outside their spheres of comfort.

It appeared that official economic growth data was based solely on the decisions and actions of those in power.

While the people suffered, the government was caught between the opposition's criticisms and the pressures exerted by international financial institutions.

The leadership was bewildered, caught in a whirlwind of confusion, and unable to devise a solution to the nation's woes.

In response, the government turned to academic and research institutions, inviting them to submit proposals to improve the country's economic conditions.

Although various proposals poured in, none of them offered sustainable solutions.

Recognising the gravity of the situation, the country's leadership decided to consult directly with selected intellectuals and visionaries for their advice. Siddique was among those invited.

The President attended the meeting with Siddique, signalling his high regard for him.

This gesture was an explicit acknowledgement of Siddique's influence and his unique perspective on societal issues.

Due to Siddique's holistic view of human life, rooted in divine guidance, he approached the problems presented with a fresh perspective.

His comprehensive understanding allowed him to easily identify the underlying factors contributing to the country's economic woes.

Siddique presented his solutions with clarity and eloquence, ensuring that even ordinary people could grasp them.

His logical and well-structured arguments were complex for anyone to dismiss.

His approach was not just to provide superficial solutions but to address the root causes, making it clear that sustainable progress could only be achieved by aligning societal values and economic policies with divine principles and ethical standards.

-

"Tell me, Siddique, what are your views on economic development?" the President asked.

Siddique took a deep breath, prepared to share his perspective.

"Mr. President, I believe that the well-being of every individual in a nation measures true progress. Economic strength and sustainability come from fair resource distribution and ensuring everyone has access to their basic and emergency needs."

The President nodded, indicating that he was following along. "How do you think this principle fits our current economic strategies?"

Siddique replied earnestly, "It aligns well with the divine order of creation. Resources are meant to sustain and fulfil the needs of the people in a particular region. However, our current system is plagued by corruption, bribery, injustice, and deceit, which undermines this principle."

The President leaned forward, interested in Siddique's proposed solutions. "So, what do you suggest we do?"

Siddique was ready with his response.

"I propose a comprehensive reform of how we utilise our resources, including human resources. We must build a system grounded in truth, honesty, transparency, accountability, and justice. This will better protect the rights and well-being of our people."

The President asked, "Are there specific practices or models you think we should adopt?"

Siddique nodded thoughtfully. "Yes, we should consider economic practices that align with Islamic teachings. These principles—fairness, equity, and ethical dealings—have proven effective throughout history in achieving social stability and economic prosperity."

"Don't you think these principles apply only to those who follow Islamic teachings?" the President inquired.

Siddique shook his head. "Not at all. The benefits of divine guidance extend to all of God's creations. Principles like justice, charity, accountability, and ethical conduct have universal applicability and can contribute to the welfare of everyone, regardless of their faith."

The President considered Siddique's words carefully. "How do you envision these reforms impacting our nation?"

Siddique's eyes shone with conviction. "We can create a more ethical governance model by adopting these reforms. This would ensure equitable resource distribution and adherence to values that promote the common good. It would uplift our nation economically, restore social harmony, and help bridge the widening gaps of inequality and injustice."

The President smiled, clearly impressed. "Thank you for sharing your perspective, Siddique. It's evident you've given these issues considerable thought."

Siddique respectfully nodded, "Thank you, Mr. President. I hope these ideas help guide us toward a more prosperous future."

--

The high-level meeting with Siddique reached the media, leading to interviews that allowed him to elaborate further on his ideas and vision for the country's development.

His words resonated deeply with many, particularly young scholars who began to look beyond his thoughts and delve into their sources—the Qur'an and the Prophet Muhammad's (PBUH) biography.

This intellectual curiosity sparked a renewed interest in understanding Islam's core teachings, leading to a significant shift in the discourse at various levels within the country.

However, Siddique's rising influence and the growing appeal of his ideas also led to conflict.

Different segments of society began to debate and clash over these perspectives.

Some media outlets, reflecting the concerns of factions, accused Siddique of being a racist, while others criticised him as a fundamentalist.

This backlash primarily came from those with a misunderstood perception of Islam or those aligned with so-called 'modernist' viewpoints that clashed with Siddique's ideas.

Despite the criticisms, Siddique, known for his ability to find opportunities in adversity, tactfully navigated these challenges.

This was evident in how he responded to one of the popular interviews he faced.

-

Interviewer: *"Siddique, you've been vocal about the need for unity and collective action in solving our nation's problems. Could you elaborate on what you mean by this?"*

Siddique: *"Certainly. My message is straightforward: anyone who truly desires progress for our country has a moral obligation to contribute, regardless of their background or beliefs. We all have a role in addressing our nation's challenges."*

Interviewer: *"You've emphasised the importance of sincerity in contributing to the nation. Can you tell us more about that?"*

Siddique: *"Yes, everyone should come forward sincerely to support the country based on their knowledge, thoughts, and beliefs. It's about actively participating in improving our society in any way we can."*

Interviewer: *"In a recent public statement, you mentioned doing your part for the country. What did you mean by that?"*

Siddique: *"As someone born and raised here, I am contributing my share by sharing my ideas openly. It's now up to the government and the people to either embrace or disregard these proposals."*

Interviewer: *"How do you view the proposals and initiatives you've put forward?"*

Siddique: *"Each proposal and initiative is a step toward realising my vision of a flourishing nation. This vision has been deeply rooted in my subconscious since childhood. I hope these ideas will contribute to a better future for our country."*

Interviewer: *"There has been a lot of debate and criticism surrounding your views. Some media outlets have accused you of being a racist, while others label you a fundamentalist. How do you respond to these accusations?"*

Siddique: *"These accusations reflect a misunderstanding of my position and intentions. I believe in promoting unity and understanding among all segments of society, and my views are rooted in principles of fairness and justice as guided by my values. Misunderstandings often arise from a lack of knowledge about the principles I advocate."*

Interviewer: *"You've faced criticism from those who misunderstand Islam and from modernist viewpoints. Can you clarify what your views on Islam and modernism are?"*

Siddique: *"Islam, as I understand and practice it, promotes justice, equality, and respect for all individuals. My stance is not against modernity but rather against misinterpretations of Islamic teachings. Modernism and progress should not come at the expense of ethical and moral principles. I aim to integrate traditional values with modern progress in a balanced and respectful manner."*

Interviewer: *"How do you address the concerns of those who believe your views are outdated or in conflict with modern values?"*

Siddique: *"It's important to distinguish between traditional values and outdated practices. My views advocate for ethical principles that are timeless and universally applicable. I encourage dialogue and open discussion to address concerns and find common ground that respects traditional values and modern advancements."*

Interviewer: *"What do you think is the root of the backlash you're facing from various societal factions?"*

Siddique: *"The backlash often stems from a lack of understanding or misinterpretation of my ideas. Some may see my emphasis on traditional values as a threat to modernity, while others might misinterpret my commitment to Islamic principles as rigid or exclusionary. I aim to foster a constructive dialogue that bridges these gaps and promotes mutual respect."*

Interviewer: *"Given the criticism, how do you plan to continue advocating for your views?"*

Siddique: *"I remain committed to my principles and will continue to advocate for them through constructive dialogue and engagement. I believe in addressing concerns with patience and clarity, and I am always open to discussing and explaining my views to those who seek to understand them better."*

Interviewer: *"Finally, what message would you like to convey to those criticising your approach?"*

Siddique: *"I would like to convey that my approach is grounded in a genuine desire to contribute positively to society. I encourage critics to engage in open dialogue and consider my views' underlying principles. Constructive criticism is welcome but should be based on understanding the discussed ideas."*

-

Similar interviews were conducted, and Siddique addressed all of them confidently.

By that time, he was not alone. A team was already formed around him to defend and promote his ideals effectively.

"My dear brother! "You must be aware of the current situation in our country." Uncle was expecting my feedback.

I immediately summarised the news updates I had read before I departed.

There's been a significant shift politically.

The government has become much more transparent and accountable.

Once rampant corruption has been drastically reduced thanks to new reforms and stringent anti-corruption measures.

The political environment is much more stable, with fair elections and active participation from diverse political parties.

The political landscape now thrives on trust and genuine representation.

Economically, the country has seen impressive growth.

The GDP has increased substantially, and the economic policies implemented have fostered innovation and entrepreneurship.

The focus on equitable resource distribution has helped uplift many communities, and poverty rates have been significantly reduced.

Economic stability has also attracted foreign investments, further boosting the country's financial health.

Things have also improved remarkably on the social front.

Society is more cohesive, with renewed unity and cooperation among its people.

Social justice has been a priority, and efforts to ensure equal opportunities for all, regardless of background, have paid off.

There's a strong sense of community, and programs to reduce inequality have successfully made significant impacts.

Educational development is another area in which the country has made great strides.

The education system has been revamped to meet international standards.

Schools and universities now have modern facilities, emphasising critical thinking and practical skills.

Students receive a high-quality education that prepares them well for the global job market.

Finally, in terms of international image, the country has earned much respect on the global stage.

Its commitment to ethical practices and development has drawn positive attention from other nations.

There are more international collaborations and partnerships, and the country is viewed as a progressive and reliable ally in global affairs.

Overall, I see a remarkable transformation in the country, making it a model of progress and stability in the modern world.

While I was completing my observations, Uncle had already started to make Dua by raising his hands.

He continued ...

"Brother, you must understand that these changes come at a cost that not everyone sees or acknowledges."

"They are built on the sacrifices of those who dedicated their lives to a vision of a 'flourishing nation' where justice prevails and every citizen, regardless of race or religion, feels a sense of belonging and responsibility."

"Those champions who worked with conviction were often misunderstood, sometimes even ridiculed. Yet, they persevered because they believed in a higher purpose."

His words were full of wisdom, and I could feel the emotion behind them.

He continued his voice now steady but filled with sincerity.

"Many of those great souls are no longer with us. They have returned to their Creator, but their legacy lives on."

"The peace, unity, and sense of responsibility growing in our society today are fruits of their labour, prayers, and unwavering commitment to the truth."

"They planted the seeds of change in the hearts and minds of people, especially the youth, and now we are beginning to see those seeds bear fruit."

He paused for a moment, his eyes still glistening with tears.

"But, my dear brother," he said softly, "the work is far from over. The journey to build a just and compassionate society is a continuous one. It requires us to play our part—to carry forward the torch they have lit."

"We must be vigilant and wise, for many forces still seek to divide us, to drag us back into the darkness of ignorance and hatred."

As he spoke, I felt a fire kindling in my heart. His words were not just a reminder but a call to action.

"May Allah grant us the strength," I said, "to continue this journey, to uphold the values of truth, justice, and compassion that those before us fought for."

Uncle nodded, his expression softening as he saw the determination in my eyes. "Indeed, my brother," he said.

"And may Allah guide us all in this noble endeavour."

Then, he continued ...

His voice trembled slightly, revealing the weight of his emotions.

"Brother," he continued, "those who remained steadfast in their mission, who did not succumb to the pressures and temptations of this world—those who truly understood their purpose."

They realised that life is more than rituals and personal acts of worship. They embraced the essence of Islamic teaching—living for the welfare of others, striving for justice, and building a society where everyone can thrive.

His eyes were fixed on me, filled with a sense of urgency. "But sadly," he said, "many have lost that understanding."

"They've been swayed by the illusion that their duty ends with personal acts of worship."

"The concept that our faith encompasses every aspect of life, including governance, justice, and social welfare, has been overshadowed by narrow interpretations and worldly distractions."

I nodded, absorbing his words.

He sighed deeply and continued,

"The good-minded leaders who once stood for justice, equality, and unity were weakened by internal conflicts, political pressures, and societal divisions."

"Their initial vigour was diluted by the struggles they faced. But even then, there were those among them who refused to be silenced, who continued to raise their voices against injustice, even when it meant standing alone."

He paused, his eyes searching mine. "You see, brother," he said, "the path of righteousness is not easy. It requires immense patience, wisdom, and resilience."

"It requires a deep understanding of our faith and a commitment to its principles, not just in words but actions."

"And the religious people?" I asked again, wanting to understand his whole perspective.

He shook his head slowly.

"Many religious people have confined themselves to the mosques, limiting their understanding of Islam to rituals and personal piety."

"While those acts are indeed important, they have overlooked the broader teachings that compel us to be proactive in society—to fight against corruption, to stand for the oppressed, to contribute to the welfare of our nation."

"For many, the fundamental belief is that 'I am a responsible citizen of this country! As a Muslim, I must help build this nation by eliminating its problems! I have no other job here!' was forgotten."

But then, he tried to express his feelings emotionally.

After a brief silence, he raised his arms and said, "Oh Allah! Bless those who lived and died intending to fulfil your wishes on this earth! Join them with those who have received your blessings."

--

As the country veered toward a devastating collapse, a sense of urgency gripped some social organisations and well-intentioned individuals.

They understood the gravity of the situation and knew they had to act decisively to safeguard the future of the next generations.

The situation was dire, and there was a strong belief that every effort must be made to protect the well-being of the nation's children and ensure their future.

Amidst this growing concern, the Nation Development Organisation was established, thanks to the tireless efforts of these forward-thinking organisations and visionaries.

Siddique was chosen to serve on the executive committee of this newly formed organisation.

The committee comprised representatives from various religions and included many individuals deeply committed to social development.

Siddique was acutely aware of the immense responsibility that came with this role.

He saw it not merely as a position but as a profound privilege and an extraordinary opportunity to make a significant impact.

Feeling the weight of this responsibility, Siddique turned to Allah, seeking strength and guidance to fulfil his duties effectively.

The public perception of Siddique was overwhelmingly positive, crucial to the project's grand launch.

The media spotlight and support from prominent alternative religious leaders helped unite various social institutions with sincere intentions.

These leaders strategically brought these institutions to the forefront, capturing the public's attention and generating a sense of hope.

The launch of the organisation was met with widespread enthusiasm. It was a beacon of hope for those who had lost faith in the country's direction and way of life.

Many viewed the organisation as a reflection of their aspirations and a symbol of their dreams for a better future.

Siddique also attended the first media conference. Although he was an ordinary executive council member, the President invited him to attend.

-

Moderator: *Good afternoon, everyone. Thank you for joining us today for this important media conference.*

The National Development Organization has a president, secretary general, and ex-com members.

The discussion will revolve around recent developments and the crucial role of the National Development Organization, especially given the country's critical situation.

We invite our esteemed media representatives to pose their questions.

Media: *President, given the core objectives of the Nation Development Organisation?*

President: *First, thank you for the opportunity to introduce this strategic initiative.*

Our objective can be summarised as four points: Fostering understanding and trust, instilling fundamental values, encouraging social work, and creating a social model that could serve as an example for neighbouring countries.

We plan to implement various actions to ensure our objectives are met and that they are at the developing stage.

Media: *My question is directed towards you, Mr. Siddique. Some* *have criticised the Nation Development Organisation as overly conservative and incompatible with modernist values.*

How do you address concerns that the organisation may hinder progressive changes needed for the country's development?

Siddique: *Thank you for the question. It's important to clarify that the Nation Development Organisation was established to address the nation's urgent needs and secure a better future for our children.*

While our approach is grounded in traditional values, it aims to ensure social justice, equitable resource distribution, and a better quality of life for everyone.

We believe modern progress can and should be achieved within a framework that respects and incorporates our core values, promoting ethical and sustainable development.

Media: *Secretary General, considerable debate has been about the organisation's inclusivity.*

Critics argue that its reliance on specific traditional frameworks may alienate society's younger, more progressive segments.

What steps are being taken to ensure that the organisation is genuinely inclusive and represents all voices?

Secretary-General: *Thank you for raising this point. The Nation Development Organisation is committed to inclusivity.*

Our executive committee includes representatives from various religions and backgrounds.

The goal is to unite different perspectives and work together towards common objectives.

We are continuously engaging with various community groups, including youth and progressive sectors, to ensure that the organisation's initiatives resonate broadly and are responsive to the needs of all citizens.

Media: *Mr. Siddique, can you provide some insight into how the Nation Development Organisation plans to handle the criticism it has faced from different factions?*

What is your strategy for addressing these concerns and moving forward?

Siddique: *Certainly. We understand that any transformative initiative will face scrutiny and diverse opinions.*

Our strategy involves maintaining an open dialogue with all stakeholders, addressing concerns transparently, and adapting our approaches where feasible to ensure broad-based support.

The core of our mission remains focused on addressing the critical needs of our nation and advancing a future that benefits everyone.

We are committed to listening, learning, and evolving as we move forward.

Media: *Mr. President, given the urgency that led to the formation of the Nation Development Organisation, what are some of the immediate actions or milestones you envision for the organisation in the coming months?*

President: *The Nation Development Organisation's immediate focus is on implementing critical initiatives that address pressing issues, such as poverty alleviation and education reform, common to everyone in the country.*

We are setting up task forces to expedite these actions and ensure effective execution.

We aim to demonstrate tangible results and build momentum towards long-term sustainable development.

We will also monitor progress closely and adjust our strategies as needed to achieve our objectives.

Media: *Mr. Siddique, reflecting on the initial launch of the Nation Development Organisation, how do you assess its impact on public perception and its role in restoring hope among the people?*

Siddique: *The launch of the Nation Development Organisation was met with tremendous enthusiasm and hope from the public.*

It represented a turning point for many who had lost faith in the country's direction.

By aligning with traditional values and modern needs, the organisation has captured the public's imagination and rallied support.

The positive public perception is a testament to the collective efforts of all involved, and we are committed to building on this momentum to achieve our vision of a prosperous and equitable nation.

Moderator: *Thank you for your thoughtful questions and insightful responses.*

This concludes our media conference. We appreciate your participation and look forward to the Nation Development Organisation's continued progress.

-

However, despite the initial excitement and promising start, the National Development Organisation faced significant challenges. Within a few months, the organisation encountered severe obstacles.

Radical racists and self-serving politicians, who were opposed to any progress, conspired to undermine the organisation's efforts.

Siddique, however, was not naive about these challenges. His visionary leadership was evident in his determination to keep the organisation's spirit alive despite the setbacks.

Even when the organisation seemed to falter, Siddique's commitment remained unwavering.

He continued to work tirelessly to prevent the organisation from fading into obscurity.

He envisioned the substantial positive changes that the organisation could bring to the country and formulated plans to realise those goals.

Siddique maintained close contact with the organisation's higher-ups, ensuring that progress continued despite the difficulties.

A year passed, and it was time for the National Development Organisation's annual meeting.

The organisation's performance had been underwhelming, leading to disappointment among attendees.

The leadership team, frustrated by the lack of progress, was reluctant to continue.

-

The National Development Organisation's annual general meeting began with tension, reflecting the organisation's recent struggles.

The leadership and various members and supporters had gathered to assess the past year's disappointing performance.

Frustration was evident on many faces, and it wasn't long before the atmosphere grew heated.

The president stood at the podium, addressing the room. He acknowledged the dissatisfaction among the attendees.

"Ladies and gentlemen," he began, "thank you all for joining us today. As you're aware, our organisation has faced significant challenges over the past year."

"The performance has not met our expectations; understandably, many of you are disappointed."

"The progress has been slower than anticipated, leading to frustration among our leadership team. Some have even questioned whether we should continue with the current approach."

A senior leadership team member was the first to respond, voicing the discontent that had been building for months.

"It's more than just slow progress, Mr. President," he said.

"We've been stagnant. The initiatives we planned haven't moved forward, and there's been a lack of clear communication between the leadership and the rest of the members. We need to face the reality that our current strategies have failed."

The president, though calm, seemed taken aback by the directness of the critique.

Another member quickly chimed in, echoing the sentiment.

"I agree. I've spoken to several members who feel disengaged. They don't see any real direction from the top. We're losing support from the grassroots, and that's dangerous for an organisation like ours."

The president tried to defend the leadership's position.

"I understand your frustrations," he said, "but we've faced unprecedented challenges, and we must consider that."

"The pandemic, political instability, and economic crises have all affected our ability to execute the plans."

But his words did little to soothe the growing discontent.

A frustrated attendee stood up and addressed the room, his voice tinged with anger.

"But that doesn't excuse the leadership's failure to adapt. Every organisation has faced difficulties, but successful ones have managed to pivot and find new ways forward."

"We've been stuck, and it's not just external factors—it's poor leadership. We can't just blame the circumstances."

The criticisms continued to pour in.

"Exactly," another member added.

"The leadership team hasn't shown any real transparency or accountability. We don't know where the funds are being

allocated, what progress we've made, or even what the next steps are."

Sensing the gravity of the situation, the president tried to steer the conversation back to a more positive tone.

"Let's not forget the initial successes we had. Yes, we've faced difficulties, but the vision remains intact. Perhaps we need fresh leadership, but let's not lose sight of what we've already accomplished."

Then, one of the organisation's founders, a respected and seasoned figure, rose to speak.

His voice carried the weight of authority.

"With all due respect, Mr. President," he said, "we're not questioning the vision; we're questioning how it's being executed."

"The disconnect between the leadership and the members is palpable. We need a new approach, direction, and perhaps leadership."

His words struck a chord with the room, and murmurs of agreement rippled through the crowd.

One critical member added, "That's exactly the issue—poor leadership. We've been let down and are on the verge of collapse. It's time for accountability, and it's time for change."

Another member nodded in agreement.

"We cannot afford to let this organisation fail, but if we continue like this, we're heading for disaster. We must bring in someone who can rebuild trust and inspire action."

The president, realising the gravity of the situation, asked a pointed question.

"What are you suggesting, then?"

"If we're to change leadership, we need a candidate who can unite us and push forward with the vision we all believe in."

"We need someone with a clear track record of getting things done."

The founder spoke again, his voice calm but resolute.

"I propose Siddique for the role of Secretary-General. He has shown unwavering commitment and vision for this organisation."

"His ability to connect with people from all walks of life is what we need right now. He's also been vocal about the need for reform and transparency—things this organisation desperately requires."

There was a pause as the room absorbed the proposal.

One sceptical attendee spoke up.

"But Siddique has only been just as a committee member. How do we know he has the experience to turn things around?"

The founder responded confidently.

"Siddique has demonstrated leadership in various capacities, nationally and internationally."

"His ability to network, communicate, and inspire is unparalleled. This organisation might need his approach to pull itself out of stagnation."

A member who supported Siddique added,

"I agree. Siddique brings a new perspective. The mistakes of the past do not bog him down. He's shown he can lead with integrity and proven his commitment to our mission."

The president looked around the room, sensing that the moment of decision had arrived.

"So, if there are no further objections, I propose we vote on Siddique's nomination as the new Secretary-General."

The room fell silent as the vote was cast. Siddique was unanimously elected as the new Secretary-General when the results came in.

The president, relieved by the outcome, smiled as he addressed Siddique.

"Congratulations, Siddique. We have full faith in your leadership. This marks the beginning of a new chapter for our organisation. Let's work together to make sure we can deliver on the promises we've made."

Siddique, feeling the weight of the responsibility, nodded.

"Thank you all. I accept this responsibility with humility and determination. With Allah's grace and the support of all of you, we will overcome these challenges."

"Let's start by reconnecting with our members, re-establishing transparency, and setting achievable goals. Together, we can turn this around."

As the meeting ended, there was a renewed sense of hope in the room. Though the road ahead remained uncertain, Siddique's election marked the start of a new era for the National Development Organisation, one filled with potential and the promise of better days ahead.

--

This began a new chapter in his ambitious journey of Siddique and the National Development Organization.

Thanks to his parents' nurturing and relentless efforts, he developed skills and traits that became invaluable assets in his role.

The guidance from the Islamic movement provided him with the necessary encouragement and motivation to pursue his ideals.

Internationally, Siddique was recognised for his exceptional abilities and high-level connections.

May Allah bless him and forgive his mistakes, both intentional and unintentional.

With Allah's grace, Siddique's leadership was accepted and supported by its members, supporters, and admirers, regardless of their background.

They rallied behind him, united in their mission, even though the path ahead was fraught with challenges.

The hard-line racists and egotistical figures, connected to some ministers with extreme views, saw the organisation as a direct threat.

They mounted severe countermeasures against Siddique and his team.

Nevertheless, Siddique and his supporters turned every obstacle into an opportunity to demonstrate their capabilities.

Over the years, they faced various ups and downs but remained steadfast in their commitment.

Siddique's leadership and personal qualities earned him respect even from those who initially opposed him.

The core objectives of the National Development Organisation were:

- To foster mutual understanding and trust among the country's people.
- To instil the fundamental values of doing good and preventing evil.
- To encourage participation in social work among good individuals.
- To create a model social order that could serve as an example for neighbouring countries.

Gradually, there was a noticeable shift in people's attitudes and behaviours towards these goals.

The changes were unstoppable, and those who had previously tried to obstruct progress could not continue.

Many of these individuals were eventually compelled to align with the rising tide of transformation.

Even during election campaigns, many had no choice but to highlight these changes as central issues.

The television debate between the two presidential candidates was one of the year's most anticipated events.

Both men were eager to prove how closely their manifestos aligned with the National Development Organisation (NDO), which had become a symbol of hope under Siddique's leadership.

The organisation's mission—to foster mutual understanding, promote social good, and create a model society—was front and centre in the discussion.

--

The moderator kicked off the debate, setting the stage.

"Tonight, we'll hear from both candidates on how to align their vision with the NDO's objectives. Let's start with Candidate A."

Candidate A, known for his calm and measured approach, opened with praise for Siddique and the NDO.

"First, let's give credit where it's due. The National Development Organisation, under Siddique's leadership, has brought people together like never before."

"My goal is to build on their success. My administration will focus on expanding social programs and giving every citizen a role in our nation's progress."

His words were met with polite applause, but there was a sense that the audience was waiting for something a bit more... lively.

The moderator smiled and turned to Candidate B.

Candidate B, never one to shy away from a fight, wasted no time.

"Let's be real," he said, leaning into his microphone.

"The NDO has done fantastic work, but they've had to deal with racists, egotists, and extremists trying to tear them down."

"My plan? Clear the path. We won't sit around and let these people get in the way."

"I'll stand with Siddique and his team, but I'll also ensure the forces trying to sabotage us are removed. It's time to stop playing nice."

The room buzzed as Candidate B's fiery remarks hit home. One viewer quipped on social media, "If debates had fireworks, B would've set the studio on fire!"

The moderator interjected, trying to keep things civil. "Both of you support the NDO, but how will you handle the opposition they've faced from within the government?"

Candidate A, ever the diplomat, responded first.

"The opposition is tough, no doubt. But when change is happening, some will resist. We need to bring everyone to the table, even those who disagree. Dialogue is key."

Candidate B wasn't buying it.

"Dialogue is nice in theory. But we've been having 'dialogues' for years. And guess what?"

"Those same old folks are still blocking progress."

"My administration won't be about endless talks. We need to act, and we need to act now. Enough with tea and biscuits!"

The audience chuckled at the jab, and Candidate A raised an eyebrow. "I happen to like tea," he quipped dryly. "But it's clear my opponent prefers coffee—strong and bitter."

Candidate B grinned, happy to play along.

"Coffee is for people who want to wake up and get things done. But if you want to sip tea and talk, be my guest!"

The debate shifted gears as the candidates discussed their broader visions for the nation.

Candidate A focused on reform, emphasising the importance of slow but steady progress.

Conversely, Candidate B clarified he was ready for radical change, even if it meant ruffling feathers.

By the end of the debate, it was clear that both candidates were focused on the same goal: aligning their policies with the NDO's mission.

Candidate A believed in diplomacy and gradual progress, while Candidate B was all about decisive action and breaking down barriers.

As the moderator thanked the candidates, he couldn't resist a parting joke.

"Well, folks, it looks like one candidate is brewing a change with tea and the other is brewing coffee. Either way, we'll all need something strong to handle the challenges ahead!"

The audience laughed, and as the cameras panned out, viewers were left with a sense that no matter who won, the National Development Organisation had already sparked a movement that was impossible to ignore. Whether through tea or coffee, progress was brewing.

-

Political parties approached Siddique, offering him ministerial positions in exchange for his support.

However, Siddique was astute enough to recognise the ulterior motives behind their offers.

Siddique played a monumental role in the country's transformation.

His dedication and trials were immense, and his efforts were pivotal in driving the nation toward positive change.

--

"He, too, has now found his peace."

"May Allah grant him the heavenly pleasures He promised His faithful servants."

With a soft and heartfelt voice, I murmured, "Ya Allah! Forgive Siddique's mistakes and bless his soul."

Siddique's life experiences are invaluable lessons for me.

I've read extensively about child-rearing and social upliftment. Yet, none of those readings conveyed the realistic understanding I am experiencing now.

This history will serve as a guiding light for people like me and will shape various turns in my life. Insha Allah!

As I spoke, I noticed a shift in my tone and breathing rhythm, reflecting Siddique's story's impact on me.

"Ya Allah!"

Show us the straight path!

Guide us in the path of good people who have received Your love and grace!

Protect us from the path of those who have received Your wrath go astray.

Ameen.

LESSONS LEARNED

The meeting I had with the uncle of my beloved friend Siddique was an extraordinary experience.

I never expected to meet him at the funeral ground. It was a great blessing from almighty Allah.

I intended to attend the funeral prayer. However, He blessed me with this opportunity to learn the life story of my respected brother, Siddique.

Based on what I learned from him, I am happy to note some key points that can help the readers.

In the meantime, you can also write about what you learned from this amazing story.

I want to provide my notes as a checklist so you can self-assess and prepare an action plan to improve your Parenting Leadership experiences to the next level.

I am giving you three checklists below:

- ☐ Root Checklist to help parents to improve their parenting experience.
- ☐ Sprout Checklist to help youth enhance their productivity.
- ☐ Tree Checklist to help community workers/leaders make their contributions effective.

ROOT CHECKLIST

Spiritual and Emotional Development		
1	I deeply connect with my spiritual practices, as Abdullah does in his prayers.	
2	I seek guidance through prayer or reflection when facing life's challenges.	
3	I feel/felt the responsibility and blessing of the almighty of having a child.	
4	Often, I appreciate moments of peace and reflection.	
5	I balance my responsibilities with caring for my emotional well-being, as Abdullah does.	
6	I am clear on my life mission and purpose, as Abdullah was.	
7	I express gratitude for the blessings in my life, just as Abdullah did.	
8	I consider the long-term impact of my values and beliefs when making significant life choices.	
9	I make supplications or pray regularly for guidance and blessings, especially concerning my family.	
10	I cultivate a more profound sense of God-consciousness (Taqwa) in myself and my family.	

Parenting and Family Environment		
11	I nurture a bond of affection and kindness between my children to ensure they grow harmoniously.	
12	I am mindful of balancing healthy competition with fostering love and kindness among my children.	
13	I use various effective strategies to help my children excel without creating jealousy or rivalry.	
14	I guide my children to see success not as outperforming others but as uplifting one another.	
15	I use daily duas and simple acts of worship to naturally teach my children about faith and good deeds.	
16	I ensure my children's education empowers them to contribute meaningfully to society.	
17	Am I shaping my children's character through stories and conversations on virtues and faith?	
18	I consciously invest time and energy in my children's development, understanding the long-term benefits of these efforts.	
19	I prepare my child or future children to welcome new siblings with love and care, as Siddique's parents did.	
20	I express gratitude for every blessing, such as the birth of a child, and include prayers for their future well-being.	

Discipline, Values, and Behaviour		
21	I take a balanced approach to discipline, avoiding pain or fear while teaching valuable lessons about right and wrong.	
22	I model honesty to my children and ensure they trust and respect my decisions when fulfilling their wishes.	
23	I foster respect in my children for others and teach them to avoid speaking poorly of others or gossiping.	
24	I teach my children compassion for those who make mistakes or are in need rather than criticising them in front of my children.	
25	I use family mealtime to teach good manners and strengthen family bonds, and I make the most of these moments.	
26	I instilled in my children the importance of order and cleanliness and ensured they developed these habits early on.	
27	I teach my children how to behave properly, such as when visiting others' homes or handling things that belong to others.	
28	I explain to my children the value of sharing and inclusivity in a way that helps them understand and appreciate it.	
29	I promote family unity and sharing among my children; I handle situations where they need to practice selflessness.	
30	I ensure my child learns to treat everyone respectfully and kindly regardless of background.	

Social Awareness and Interaction		
31	I try to build strong friendships with families with similar values to support each other's parenting journeys.	
32	I ensure my children are exposed to good company and wise thoughts, even if they may not fully understand everything at a young age.	
33	I am creating a welcoming environment at home where my children's friends can feel safe and encouraged to adopt good values.	
34	I am mindful of who my children spend time with and ensure that positive influences surround them.	
35	I actively engage with the parents of my children's friends to promote shared values and a supportive community.	
36	Before my child, I model respectful behaviour towards people of different religions and backgrounds.	
37	I am addressing and correcting any negative attitudes or behaviours my child might exhibit towards others.	
38	I explain the value of dignity and respect in interactions with all individuals, including those in service/working roles.	
39	I create opportunities for my child to practice kindness and compassion in real-life situations.	
40	I help my child understand the rewards of showing good character and respect to others, as our faith teaches.	

Learning and Growth		
41	I help my children develop resilience and problem-solving skills through gradual challenges and guided experiences.	
42	I observe and identify my children's natural strengths and areas for growth.	
43	I balance encouragement and guidance in nurturing my children's skills while being mindful that these skills will develop over time.	
44	I help my children improve their confidence and communication skills early on.	
45	I provide exposure to different cultures in my children's everyday activities in a fun and engaging way.	
46	I tell stories to teach my children essential values, bravery, honesty, and kindness.	
47	I incorporate physical activities and games to help my children develop courage and a fearless spirit.	
48	I create opportunities for my children to express themselves and face new challenges in a supportive environment.	
49	I encourage my children to explore new things.	
50	I am providing my children various reading materials to expand their knowledge and vocabulary.	

SPROUT CHECKLIST

Encouraging Participation and Development		
1	I encourage my children to join community or educational activities like Siddique in the Islamic Children's Circles.	
2	I create opportunities for my children to build friendships in environments that promote good character and values.	
3	I ensure my children experience positive social interactions and avoid negative peer pressure.	
4	I am teaching my children to balance theory and practice in their daily actions.	
5	I help my children apply moral and ethical lessons from school to their daily lives.	
6	I instil in my children an eagerness for learning and growth like Siddique.	
7	I support my children in embracing new opportunities and stepping out of their comfort zone.	
8	I motivate my children to be active learners in educational or community programs.	
9	Like Siddique's enthusiasm, I encourage my children to be dedicated and committed to community activities.	
10	As Siddique did, I help my children discover their purpose and passion at a young age.	

Values and Responsibility		
11	I teach my children to show gratitude and appreciation for their mentors as Siddique did.	
12	As Siddique did, I help my children connect spiritually and use prayer for reflection and purpose.	
13	As Siddique did, I am instilling a sense of responsibility and community contribution in my children.	
14	I promote humility and kindness in my children, ensuring they care for the overlooked.	
15	I encourage my children to respect and value the elderly, like Siddique did.	
16	Like Siddique's dedication, I (as a youth) align my goals with societal needs.	
17	I am (as a youth) seeking inspiration and motivation from my experiences to drive my efforts.	
18	I (as a youth) strive to be a role model by embodying integrity, dedication, and purpose.	
19	I (as a youth) use community work as an opportunity for personal growth and societal contribution.	
20	I (as a youth) ensure my actions positively impact others, like Siddique's influence on his peers.	

Personal and Academic Development		
21	I (as a youth) recognise the value of small acts of kindness in making others feel valued and supported.	
22	I (as a youth) use leisure time to keep myself busy and protect myself from engaging in evil thoughts and acts.	
23	I am (as a youth) choosing recreational activities that align with my long-term objectives and skills development.	
24	I (as a youth) seek opportunities to expand my knowledge and skills across fields to enhance my future endeavours.	
25	I (as a youth) apply my academic and personal learning to contribute to my growth and others' well-being.	
26	I am (as a youth) engaging with experienced individuals to deepen my understanding and develop my ideas.	
27	I (as a youth) balance personal interests with a commitment to societal betterment, using my potential.	
28	I (as a youth) reflect on and document my learning to support continuous personal growth.	
29	I (as a youth) actively share knowledge and ideas to contribute to my community's development.	
30	Like Siddique's journey, I (as a youth) ensure my actions and achievements reflect a clear sense of purpose and impact.	

Managing Challenges and Decisions		
31	I am (as a youth) mindful of avoiding futile debates and focusing on meaningful connections and positive influence.	
32	I (as a youth) handle situations where emotions or peer pressure sway me.	
33	I (as a youth) am open to understanding different perspectives and avoiding harsh criticism of societal or traditional practices.	
34	I (as a youth) balance my desires with the Islamic principles I've learned, especially during challenging times.	
35	I (as a youth) remind myself of my core values and Islamic teachings during temptation or doubt.	
36	I (as a youth) actively seek opportunities to impact rather than waiting for the right moment positively.	
37	I (as a youth) ensure my actions reflect my values, even when faced with immediate gratification.	
38	I (as a youth) am aware of how my choices align with my long-term goals and who I want to become.	
39	I (as a youth) maintain God-consciousness and accountability, especially when away from parental or community supervision.	
40	I (as a youth) am managing my finances responsibly, tracking expenses, and living within my means.	

Growth, Support, and Leadership		
41	I (as a youth) balance my freedom with upholding my values and principles.	
42	I (as a youth) am actively practising self-discipline to handle responsibilities and challenges of independence.	
43	I (as a youth) regularly reflect on my personal growth and the impact of my actions on my goals.	
44	I (as a youth) seek support or guidance when struggling to stay true to my principles or manage responsibilities.	
45	I (as a youth) am consciously using my knowledge and skills to benefit others and contribute to community change.	
46	I (as a youth) incorporate regular practices, like fasting, to manage my desires and stay focused on my goals.	
47	I (as a youth) turn to my faith or beliefs for strength when facing challenges, as Siddique did.	
48	I (as a youth) am prepared to handle significant responsibilities with composure during personal or family crises.	
49	I (as a youth) support and guide others effectively during challenging times, as Siddique did when his dad passed away.	
50	I (as a youth) stay committed to my studies and personal development amidst distractions or peer pressure.	

TREE CHECKLIST

(CW/L – Community Worker/Leader)

Community Harmony and Leadership		
1	I (as a CW/L) address divisive ideas or external influences that threaten community harmony while respecting all perspectives.	
2	I (as a CW/L) ensure my actions contribute to unity rather than division in times of tension.	
3	I (as a CW/L) use public speaking to promote positive values and address critical issues constructively.	
4	I (as a CW/L) balance advocating for progress with preserving traditional values in my community.	
5	I (as a CW/L) respond to criticisms of cultural or religious practices while upholding community cohesion.	
6	I (as a CW/L) remain composed when addressing challenging topics in public forums.	
7	I (as a CW/L) inspire others to engage in dialogue that aligns with the values of peace and understanding.	
8	I (as a CW/L) turn to my core beliefs for guidance in conflict situations.	
9	I (as a CW/L) support others in developing the courage to stand up for shared values.	
10	I (as a CW/L) ensure my leadership style fosters community unity and addresses grievances.	

Tradition vs. Modernity and Family Support		
11	I (as a CW/L) understand how well I do traditional customs, and I examine outdated practices.	
12	I (as a CW/L) critically evaluated traditional practices that may be irrational. I am willing to discuss these with the right people.	
13	I (as a CW/L) promote a balanced view of modernism and tradition within my community.	
14	In times of social upheaval, I am (as a CW/L) skilful at managing conflicts and divisions within the community.	
15	I (as a CW/L) support families in remaining solid and harmonious.	
16	I (as a CW/L) combat moral decay and negative trends among youth.	
17	I (as a CW/L) am involved in advocating for family and community values in education.	
18	I am (as a CW/L) proactive in organising workshops for newly married couples.	
19	I (as a CW/L) use media to promote positive family values and societal norms.	
20	I am (as a CW/L) actively identifying and regulating literature or media that undermines family values.	

Societal Issues and Personal Growth		
21	I am (as a CW/L) prepared to respond to societal crises that affect the community.	
22	I (as a CW/L) effectively educate about maintaining a balance between tradition and modernity.	
23	I (as a CW/L) guide the community through challenging times with clear, compassionate leadership.	
24	I (as a CW/L) listen to and address the concerns of different generations within the community.	
25	I am (as a CW/L) committed to personal growth as a community leader.	
26	I (as a CW/L) address societal issues comprehensively, addressing root causes.	
27	I (as a CW/L) ensure my approach aligns with universal values such as justice and compassion.	
28	I (as a CW/L) incorporate fair resource distribution and well-being into my work.	
29	I (as a CW/L) take steps to combat corruption and promote transparency.	
30	I (as a CW/L) advocate for ethical practices in my professional and personal interactions.	

Media Influence and Advocacy		
31	I (as a CW/L) carefully address criticism or backlash when my views clash with others.	
32	I (as a CW/L) leverage media to spread my message and influence public discourse.	
33	I (as a CW/L) inspire young scholars to explore core values related to my advocacy.	
34	I (as a CW/L) find and create opportunities during adversity or conflict.	
35	I (as a CW/L) contribute to societal debates in a way that fosters understanding and constructive dialogue.	
36	I (as a CW/L) develop and communicate a clear vision for societal or organisational change.	
37	I (as a CW/L) ensure my actions reflect personal integrity and consistency with my values.	
38	I (as a CW/L) balance respecting cultural traditions with promoting necessary progress and reform.	
39	I (as a CW/L) deeply understand the broader purpose of my role beyond personal acts of service.	
40	I (as a CW/L) address societal issues holistically, considering immediate needs and long-term solutions.	

Justice, Equality, and Application of Faith		
41	I am (as a CW/L) committed to pursuing equality in my community.	
42	I (as a CW/L) handle internal conflicts, political pressures, and societal divisions in my work.	
43	I (as a CW/L) apply my faith's broader teachings to address community issues.	
44	I (as a CW/L) ensure my actions align with the principles of justice.	
45	I (as a CW/L) handle criticism or opposition without compromising my integrity.	
46	I (as a CW/L) promote transparency and accountability in the systems I work with.	
47	I (as a CW/L) manage divisions within the community effectively.	
48	I (as a CW/L) balance ritualistic practices with proactive societal engagement.	
49	I (as a CW/L) leverage my leadership role to guide the community through challenges.	
50	I (as a CW/L) support and mentor others to develop courage and clarity of vision.	

ABOUT THE AUTHOR

Dr. Mohamed Nismy is a human resource development strategist, author, accomplished trainer, leadership coach, and management consultant with over two decades of experience. With a professional foundation as a Civil Engineer, he has spent more than ten years contributing to the Oil and Gas industry, holding key positions such as Quality Assurance Engineer and Strategic Business Planner.

His academic journey is marked by a commitment to excellence, holding both B.Sc. and M.Sc. Degrees in Engineering. However, his thirst for knowledge led him to pursue higher education, obtaining an MBA (UK) and an MA (IOU). A pivotal chapter in his academic career unfolded at the University of Malaya (UM), where he completed his PhD, focusing on the "Identification of Talents for Effective Utilization of People." Presently, Dr. Mohamed Nismy holds the esteemed position of an Elite Fellow at UM.

Dr. Mohamed Nismy is a certified life coach, executive coach, and leadership coach from the esteemed Certified Coaches Federation in Canada and an accredited professional advanced trainer by the Institute of Leadership and Management (ILM) in the UK.

The amalgamation of his multi-disciplinary qualifications uniquely positions him to offer transformative training and consulting services to professionals and businesses of diverse backgrounds. Dr Mohamed Nismy's specialisation lies in sustainable Human Resources Development, and his expertise spans Strategic Planning.

His impact extends far and wide. He has positively influenced thousands of individuals through tailor-made training and coaching programs and conducts corporate training programs covering various topics.

Beyond the corporate arena, Dr. Mohamed Nismy dedicates time to individual coaching programs designed to meet the specific needs of diverse groups. For entrepreneurs, he imparts wisdom on effective business leadership; for young leaders, he offers strategic leadership; for professionals, he guides the path to career success; and for students, he provides invaluable insights into educational and career paths.

Dr. Mohamed Nismy Rafiudeen combines academic prowess with practical experience, offering a holistic approach to leadership development. His commitment to empowering individuals, regardless of their background, is evident in his diverse portfolio of training and coaching programs.

LM GLOBAL CONSULTANCY

Your HR Development Partner

Everyone has unique built-in potential, which could be capitalised on through effective training, coaching, and consultation to become a G*lobal Mind*.

A Global Mind is an individual who recognises and utilises the built-in potential to demonstrate extraordinary performance in their profession and achieve a successful life enriched with Universal Values.

At Leaders Mind Global, we employ all the best possible techniques to identify your potential and readiness to facilitate your development roadmap with solid measures.

We specialise in providing Training, Coaching, and Management Consultancy services. We empower people and businesses to achieve sustainable development by optimally using their innate potential.

We envision a productive work culture where leaders and professionals thrive and are committed to achieving excellence. Our firm belief that "Will to good change is the way to success" motivates us to leave no stone unturned in ensuring the success of our clients.

www.leadersmindglobal.com

www.ingramcontent.com/pod-product-compliance
Ingram Content Group UK Ltd.
Pitfield, Milton Keynes, MK11 3LW, UK
UKHW021406190726
13845UKWH00028B/906